Nineteen Centuries of the Christian Church

Daniel Webster Kurtz, M. A., D. D.

Author of "An Outline of Fundamental Doctrines of Faith"
President-elect of McPherson College, McPherson, Kansas

Published by the

General Sunday School Board
of the Church of the Brethren

ELGIN, ILLINOIS

Printed and Sold by
BRETHREN PUBLISHING HOUSE
ELGIN, ILL.

DEDICATED

TO

THE FRIEND OF EVERYBODY

AND

A MOTHER TO THE NEEDY AND SAD

MARY S. GEIGER

WHOSE LIFE OF FAITH, HOPE, LOVE, IS ONE OF THE
BRIGHTEST STARS IN THE HISTORY OF THE
CHRISTIAN CHURCH

THE AUTHOR'S PREFACE.

There is scarcely a paragraph in this little book where the author did not feel handicapped by the space limitations put upon him. It is extremely difficult to condense a great subject to such narrow limits and yet show the movement of history, the development of the ideas, creeds, forms and problems of the church. It has been the purpose of the author to make this work suggestive, to point out as far as possible the causes and effects of the great movements of church history.

The general scheme of the history of the church the author received from his teachers, Walker of Yale, and Harnack of Berlin. But over a hundred authorities have been consulted more or less in preparing this work. As far as possible original sources, such as the church fathers, have been used as the basis of judgment.

Recognition has been given, throughout the book, of the authors whose words have been quoted exactly. The other sources are too numerous to catalogue here.

It is suggested that the teachers of "training classes" should read larger works on the history of the Church, at least outlines such as Zenos' "Compendium of Church History," or Moncrief's " Church History," and also consult the more comprehensive works of Newman, Schaff, Hurst, " The Ten Epochs of Church History," and for some subjects the classic works of Milman and Robertson.

The size of this book is not the measure of the labor put upon it, but if it will introduce our people to a larger interest in the history of the Church, the author will feel amply repaid for his labor.

D. W. K.

June 1, 1914.

Philadelphia, Pa.

TABLE OF CONTENTS

I. The Apostolic Age, 4 B. C. to
100 A. D. 9

II. From the Apostolic Age to Constantine, 100 to 313 31

III. From Constantine to Gregory I., 315 to 590 53

IV. From Gregory to Charlemagne, 590 to 814 71

V. From Charlemagne to Gregory. VII., 814 to 1073 85

VI. From Gregory VII. to Boniface VIII., 1073 to 1294 99

VII. From Boniface VIII. to Luther's Theses, 1294 to 1517 119

VIII. The Reformation, 1517 to 1648...135

IX. The Church of the Brethren 159

X. From Kant (1780) to the Present..179

Nineteen Centuries of the Christian Church

CHAPTER I

The Apostolic Age, 4 B. C. to 100 A. D.

I. INTRODUCTION.

Church history is older and younger than Christ. In one sense the true Church of God might be traced back to the prophets. In the other sense, the Church organization began after the " resurrection faith " became the basis of the Church. Without this faith the disappointed apostles would never have united to perpetuate the life and teachings of Jesus.

Church history, proper, is the study of organized Christianity. It includes (1) Christian Life and Worship. (2) Church Extension or Missions. (3) Christian Doctrine or Theology. (4) Church Government. (5) Christian Literature.

The history of the Church, according to time, is divided into, (1) The Ancient Church, 4 B. C. to 590 A. D. (2) The Mediæval Church, 590 A. D. to 1517 A. D. (3) The Modern Church, 1517 to the present. These epochs are again divided into periods, according to the chapters of this book.

II. JUDAISM.

Before we can understand the rise of the Christian Church we must understand her background in Judaism.

1. The Old Testament was the Scriptures of the first Christians. It teaches (1) Monotheism—the God of Abraham, the Creator of all things, is also the Father of Jesus the Christ. (2) A high ethics—righteousness and holiness, which find their climax in the great prophets (Isa. 6. Mic. 6:8. Hos., Amos). Jesus was in line with the spiritual and moral teachings of the prophets, rather than a successor of the priests. (3) Forms of worship, which were developed by later Judaism into the synagogue and temple worship, forming a model for the new Church. (4) Hymnology. The Book of Psalms, the hymn book of the second temple, was inherited by the Christians. (5) The Sabbath, rites, feasts and officials.

2. The Messianic Hope. The Old Testament contains many references to the Messianic Kingdom and the coming of the Messiah, but these were more highly developed by Judaism in the apocalyptic and apocryphal literature. This strong expectation of the kingdom of God with the Messiah as King, prepared the way for Christianity.

3. The Dispersion. The Jews were scattered, in the time of Christ, over the entire Roman Empire. Everywhere they built synagogues. These synagogues were the centers of Christian missions for a century. They also became the model for the Christian Church.

III. THE ROMAN EMPIRE.

In the fullness of time Christ came (Gal. 4:4). God had prepared the world for the coming of Christ.

1. One Language. By the conquest of Alexander the Great (Battle of Arbela, 331 B. C.), the Greek language spread over the entire civilized world.

2. One Empire. By 31 B. C. the Roman Empire became universal. Universal peace reigned. The universal empire became a model for the future organization of the Church.

3. One People. Race barriers were broken down and all the provinces called themselves Roman.

4. International Traffic. The Roman roads and sea traffic were excellent, and the extensive commerce of the day caused an intermingling of races and an interchange of ideas. One Phrygian merchant (according to his tombstone) made seventy-two trips to Rome.

5. Religious Toleration. As long as religious sects made no civil disturbances they had great freedom. The Jews and Christians were not persecuted until suspected of civil opposition or national treason.

6. Decay of Other Religions. The Greek gods were discredited and their philosophies became puerile. The world despaired of salvation save by miracle or from above. People everywhere were turning to " something new." Monotheism and a higher ethics were taught by Socrates, Plato, Aristotle and the Stoics, but only the few could understand these high teachings.

7. A New Psychology. Men everywhere distinguished between soul (or spirit) and body; God and the world; knowledge and life; sin and salvation. Men began to feel their entanglement in contradicting philosophies and hopeless bondage to sin, and longed for a power from above.

IV. JOHN THE BAPTIST.

John was the last and greatest of the prophets, who announced the presence of the kingdom and the King. He taught, further, that not birth (race) but righteousness was the true condition of entrance into the new kingdom; repentance and baptism for the remission of sins; baptism, as the true symbol of a complete cleansing or change of heart; and the judgment upon those who do not repent (Luke 3:3).

V. JESUS.

The New Testament does not give us a complete biography of Jesus, but a series of character sketches. We have the events, the teachings, and the impressions of Jesus.

1. The Events of Jesus. The events of Jesus are the things which he did and the things which others did to him. (1) Born 4 B. C. at Bethlehem of Judea. (2) He grew up at Nazareth of Galilee, where he advanced in wisdom and stature, and in favor with God and men (Luke 2:52). (3) He was a devout Jew; attended the feasts at Jerusalem and the synagogue at Nazareth. To fulfill all righteousness he went to John to be baptized (Mark 1:9-11; Matt. 3:13-17). (4) His baptism and temptation were immediately followed by his entrance upon his public ministry (Mark 1:14, 15). (5) His primary work was preaching and teaching the "Gospel of the Kingdom" (Luke 4:18). (6) "Because of compassion" he healed the sick and fed the hungry, and performed other deeds of mercy (Mark 1:41; 6:34). (7) He was rejected by the Jews, was persecuted and crucified (John 19). The evening before his crucifixion he instituted the ordinances of feet-washing, the agape, and the eucharist (John 13; 1 Cor. 11. (8) His resurrection and ascension welded the disciples together into a family, transformed their waverings into a triumphant faith, and impelled them to spread his kingdom.

2. Jesus' Teaching. (1) The Fatherhood of God and the brotherhood of man in a newer and deeper sense than in the Old Testament. (2) The kingdom (reign) of God and its gradual growth from small begin-

14

nings to universal triumph (Mark 13). The kingdom of God means the spiritual reign of God in the hearts of men. The Church is the organization, the means, by which the reign of God is established in men's hearts. (3) The higher ethics and the law of love. Religion is not formalism, or worldly success, but righteousness and peace and joy in the Holy Ghost (Rom. 14: 17). "Except your righteousness exceed that of the scribes and Pharisees, ye shall in no wise enter into the kingdom of heaven" (Matt. 5:20). Love is the power by which this holy life is attained (Rom. 13: 10).

3. **The Impression Jesus Made** upon others—friends and foes. Jesus' disciples left all and followed him. Peter confessed for them all, "Thou art the Christ, the Son of the living God" (Matt. 16:16); Pilate said, "I find no fault in him" (John 19:4, 6). Jesus' own conscience never condemned him. "Which of you convicteth me of sin" (John 8:46)?

VI. THE FOUNDINGS OF THE CHURCH.

The word "Church," ecclesia, means "The called out." Paul speaks of the

Church under the figures of "a building," "the body of Christ," and also "the bride of Christ." The Church then consisted of all the disciples of Christ, called out of the world, who organized themselves together to propagate the life and teachings of Jesus. At first there was no organization; a spiritual unity with Christ as Head. All were held together by a common love and purpose. Organization came gradually.

The "invisible Church" or the reign (kingdom) of God may be larger or smaller than organized Christianity. Church history has to do only with the visible Church or the "Church militant." This got its real start or impetus at Pentecost (Acts 1 and 2). The command (Acts 1:8) was carried out. The Christians at Jerusalem worshiped in the temple, and were in most respects like Jews in their worship and life. Persecutions scattered the Christians and spread Christianity. This is one of the supreme examples where good came out of apparent evil.

VII. PAUL.

1. Paul was born in Tarsus, a Pharisee, of the tribe of Benjamin, educated in Jerusalem in the school of Gamaliel, and became a zealous persecutor of the Christians (Philpp. 3:5, 6).

2. He Consented To and Assisted in the martyrdom of Stephen, who was the real victor in the tragedy (Acts 7:58; 8:1).

3. Paul Went to Damascus with authority to persecute the Christians, and on the approach to the ancient city was converted to the Christ whom he persecuted (35-36 A. D.; Acts 9).

4. After Some Years he entered upon his great missionary career, through which the center of Christianity was transferred from Palestine to Rome (Gal. 1:17; 2:1).

5. Paul's Missionary Journeys. (1) First Journey. With Barnabas and John Mark to Cyprus and the cities of southern Galatia, Perga, Antioch, Iconium, Lystra and Derbe (Acts 13, 14; 47 A. D.). (2) Second Journey (Acts 15: 41; 16; 17; 18). Paul revisited the cities in Galatia, of the first journey, then pressed on to the northwest and came to Troas, where he received the Macedonian call. He entered Europe and visited Philippi (Acts 16: 20-40), Amphipolis (Acts 17: 1), Apollonia (Acts 17: 1), Thessalonica (Acts 17: 1-9), Berea (Acts 17: 10-13), Athens (Acts 17: 15-34), Corinth (Acts 18: 1), Cenchrea (49 A. D.; Acts

18:18), and back to Jerusalem (Acts 18:22), via Ephesus. (3) Third Journey (Acts 18:23 to 20:3). This journey (52 A. D.) covers practically the same territory as the second journey. During this journey he made his long stay at Ephesus (Acts 19:1 to 20:11). On his return to Jerusalem he went from Troas to Assos, then to Mitylene (Acts 20:4), Chios (v. 15), Samos, Trogyllium, Miletus (vs. 16-38), Coos (Acts 21:1), Rhodes, Patara, Tyre, Ptolemais (Acts 21:7), Cæsarea and Jerusalem. (4) Paul was made a prisoner at Jerusalem, and was taken to Cæsarea (Acts 23:33). Here he remained more than two years, where he was tried by Felix and Herod Agrippa (Acts 24-26). He appealed to Rome, whither he was taken, the ship touching at Zidon (Acts 27:3), Myra, Malta, Syracuse, Rhegium, Puteoli, and the Appian Way to Rome (59 A. D.). Further journeys of Paul are quite problematic and can not be discussed here. Paul was imprisoned in Rome, where, however, he had some freedom, but was finally martyred.

VIII. THE OTHER APOSTLES.

Very little is known positively about the other apostles. Only hints here and there and traditions of uncertain value are available.

1. Peter. It is generally believed that Peter suffered martyrdom at Rome 64 A. D., during the Neronian persecutions. The traditions that he was for twenty-five years Bishop of Rome are entirely untrustworthy. They arose late in the second century.

2. James, the Lord's Brother. James was Bishop of the Church at Jerusalem, where he was condemned and martyred (A. D. 61-66).

3. Others. " We know almost nothing of the career of John from the time of the Apostolic Conference, when Paul reckoned him as one of the 'pillars' of the Jerusalem Church, to the Neronian persecution. It is probable that, long before A. D. 64, he had entered upon his missionary work in the province of Asia, but his writings and the most we know of his labors are of a later date. To Jude, a brother of the Lord, a short canonical epistle is ascribed. He probably remained in connection with the Jerusalem Church. Early tradition of uncertain value represents Andrew, Matthew, and Bartholomew as laboring in the region of the Black Sea; Thomas, Thaddeus, and

Simon the Canaanite in the remote East, as far as India, and Philip in Asia Minor. We have no trustworthy accounts of the results of their labors, or the dates or circumstances of their death."* Tradition also says that Mark labored in Egypt and founded the Church at Alexandria.

IX. IMPORTANT EVENTS OF THE PERIOD.

1. Jerusalem Council (Acts 15). The mission work of the Church raised important questions of doctrine. The Jerusalem Christians continued to keep the Jewish feasts, to circumcise their children, and to comply with Jewish customs in general. These Jewish Christians (see Galatians) thought the Gentiles could become Christians only by first becoming Jews, through circumcision and the ordinary rites of making proselytes.

Paul preached that man is saved by faith, through God's grace, and that the Gentiles could come direct to Christ without the Jewish law. Paul was victorious in the conference which decided (1) To grant freedom to the Gentiles from the law. (2) To

*Newman (Ch. Hist.), Vol. I, p. 110.

call their attention to the ethical teachings of Christianity (Acts 15:20).

2. Nero's Persecutions. Nero burned the city of Rome in 64 A. D. The conflagration went far beyond his expectations, wiping out the greater part of the city, with many of its principal buildings. The people resented this, and Nero, to shift responsibility from his own shoulders, blamed the Christians for the burning of the city. No doubt Nero's wife, Poppæa, a Jewess, suggested this to him. The Christians were covered with the skins of animals and torn to pieces by dogs; and others were covered with tar and burned to light the city. It was doubtless during the Neronian persecutions that both Peter and Paul were martyred, 64-65 A. D. Nero's persecutions from 64 to 68 were indescribably horrible.

3. The Fall of Jerusalem, A. D. 70. From A. D. 44 on, the Roman procurators had been bad and avaricious men. In A. D. 66 the Jewish Zealots revolted in Cæsarea. Twenty thousand Jews were slaughtered in Cæsarea, and this resulted in a general uprising of the Jews. Fifteen thousand Jews were slaughtered in Scythopolis. Vespasian was sent by Nero, 67 A. D., to quell the rebellion. Nero died in 68, and in 69 Vespasian became emperor. His son Titus then, with an army of 80,000, besieged Jerusalem, 70 A. D. Famine, pestilence, and cannibalism added to the horrors of the siege. As soon as any part of the city fell into the hands of the Romans, the inhabitants were ruthlessly executed. Over 1,000,000 were slaughtered and 100,000 taken captive. Others were sent into slavery, and the choicest young men were compelled to enter the gladiatorial exhibitions. The temple was destroyed. The Zealots who escaped went to Alexandria and caused an insurrection there, which resulted in their destruction with the temple at Leontopolis.

The result of the fall of Jerusalem and the temple was, for Christianity, a blessing in disguise. (1) No more temple worship and Jewish formalism. (2) Christians felt that this destruction was the fulfillment of Jesus' prophecies (Matt. 21:43; 23:37-39; Luke 21:20-28). (3) It intensified the zeal of the Christians, and spiritualized their religion.

4. Persecutions of Domitian, A. D. 81 to 96. Domitian was a cruel, arrogant, autocratic emperor. He assumed the titles of

" God," " Lord and God," " Jupiter," etc.,
and demanded the people to worship the
State religion incarnated in himself. He
sent spies all over the empire and (94-96)
cruelly persecuted all who did not worship
in his name. Domitian was a second Nero
(Rev. 17: 11) in cruelty. Probably at this
time John was banished to the Isle of Pat-
mos.

X. CHURCH EXTENSION.

By the end of the first century (100 A.
D.) Christianity had spread over Judea, Sa-
maria, Syria, Asia Minor, Macedonia,
Achaia, Arabia, Italy, Egypt and North
Africa, and as far as Spain. The method
of propagation was such missionary activities as Paul's, and the rapid spread of ideas
through commerce and travel. But most of
all it was the practice of the early Christians to bear testimony to all their neighbors and friends of the power of Christ, the
resurrected Lord. **Everyone was a missionary.**

XI. LITERATURE.

When Jesus ascended, his disciples expected his speedy return. But as his second
coming was delayed they finally, for prac-

tical reasons, wrote down his words and deeds.

Scholars differ very widely as to the exact dates when the various books of the New Testament were written.

The entire New Testament was written from about 50 A. D. to 95 A. D. Paul's Epistles were written from about 50 to 65 A. D. The first three Gospels were written between 65 and 85 A. D.; John's Gospel, not before 95 A. D. The Apocalypse (Revelation) was no doubt written during the persecutions of Domitian (94-96); some think during Nero's persecutions (64-68); the Epistle of James about 61 A. D. (authorities differ from 45 to 130 A. D.); Epistle to the Hebrews, about 80 A. D.; John's Epistles about the same time as his Gospel. The date and authorship of any writing are determined by the external authorities, traditions, etc., as to when the book was quoted or used and to whom it was attributed; and also to the internal evidence of the subject matter which often refers to events or ideas which can be definitely dated. Besides the books which are now in the New Testament canon, other Gospels and Epistles were written which were not selected for the New Testament canon (Luke 1: 1).

XII. CHRISTIAN LIFE AND WOR-SHIP.

The keynote of Christianity was victory over the world and sin through faith. Even the worst enemies of the Christians testified to their pure and noble lives. Their worship was simple. There was no ritual and formalism which characterized the later Church.

Their theology was the " Theology of the Good Shepherd." Their religion was not the religion of a book, but of a Person, the living Lord. Baptism was only for believers and by trine immersion.

Their church services consisted in bearing testimony to the power of Christ in their lives, prayers and thanksgiving, hymns and psalms, and the common meal with the eucharist. An important part of all these services was the free-will offerings for the poor.

XIII. CHURCH GOVERNMENT.

As early as the Conference at Jerusalem (49-50) we find apostles, elders, and brethren working conjointly. Eph. 4:11: "And he gave some to be apostles; and some, prophets; and some, evangelists; and some, pastors and teachers." Acts 6:1-6 tells that seven men full of wisdom and of the Spirit were chosen for the work of charity.

1. Apostles (meaning of word,—"one sent," i. e., missionary). The apostles were first of all the twelve; then also others who had seen the Lord and witnessed his resurrection. Paul called himself an apostle. There was also a broader meaning, for others are called apostles, as Barnabas, Apollos, Timothy, Silvanus, Junias, etc. These were great missionaries, who went about with authority to create, advise and direct churches.

2. Prophets (forth-teller). The primary meaning of prophet is not to foretell events, but to speak forth the truth as God has revealed it directly to the conscience of the prophet. These prophets in the New Testament were evidently gifted preachers with great insight into spiritual things, who preached with power.

3. Evangelists. The evangelists were no doubt mission workers in a larger sense than the average layman, but not to the extent of the apostles. The meaning of the word is, "A preacher of the Good News."

4. Pastors and Teachers. In Eph. 4: 11 these two words are taken together, and doubtless refer to the double function of the same office. The pastor's work is to guard, feed, teach and perfect the saints, that they may do their work of ministering and building up the body of Christ. See also John 21: 15-17, " Feed my sheep."

5. Elders or Bishops. The word " elder " has a Jewish, and the word " bishop " a Greek origin. All authorities agree that in the early Church the two words—elder and bishop—referred to the same persons and offices, or at least, offices of equal rank (Acts 20: 17, 28). Their duties were to oversee the churches and administer discipline, settle disputes, conduct the public services and also supervise the charities of the Church. Later on, one of these elders became president and took the Greek name, " overseer," a bishop (overseer).

6. Deacons. (Meaning, minister.) In Acts 6, the seven men chosen were to have a particular ministry—to have charge of the charities of the Church. This soon was done by the bishop, who became treasurer of the poor-fund. The seven deacons bore testimony and preached the same as preachers. In the later Apostolic Church (1 Tim. 3) there was a board of deacons distinct from the " elders " or " bishops." Their principal function seems to have been the gathering and distributing of the charities, while the overseer (bishop) had charge of them.

XIV. THEOLOGICAL TENDENCIES.

In spite of the simple life and worship of the apostolic age, there already appeared theological tendencies which came to fruition later.

1. Dogma. The opposition and skepticism of the age demanded an intellectual proof The Epistle to the Hebrews is theological throughout. Definitions, arguments, and analogies are marshaled to defend the Gospel.

2. Sacramentalism. The symbols began to be used in a Jewish or even heathen sense; that they would by themselves work out salvation.

3. Ecclesiasticism—identifying the visible Church with the invisible body of Christ.

4. Asceticism. By the great contrast of flesh and spirit, men began to flee from the world rather than to overcome the world.

5. Chiliasm—belief that the millennium

was near at hand, and thus neglect the greater Christian duties of loving service and missionary endeavor, by lazily waiting for Christ's coming.

QUESTIONS.

1. Define Church history. Into what three epochs is it divided? What phases of Christianity does Church history treat?

2. What relation has Judaism to Christianity? Name three things that the Church inherited from the Old Testament. Name two more ways in which Judaism has paved the way for the Church.

3. What is the meaning of Gal. 4: 4? Name six ways in which God prepared the world for Christ's coming.

4. What is John the Baptist's relation to Jesus? What did he teach?

5. What do we know about Jesus? What was Jesus' primary work? Name five other events of Jesus' life. Sum up Jesus' teachings in three statements. What is the nature of the kingdom of God? What impression did Jesus make upon others?

6. Distinguish between the "visible" and "invisible" Church. Which do we study? When did the Church begin?

7. Who was Paul? What was his character? Describe his conversion. How many missionary journeys did he make and what countries did he visit?

8. Who was Peter? Where did he die? What do you know about James, the Lord's brother? Where did John do mission work?

THE APOSTOLIC AGE

9. Name four important events of this period. Describe each.

10. How did the early Christians spread their religion? How far had Christianity spread at the end of the first century?

11. When was the New Testament written? How many books of the New Testament were written by missionaries? How many epistles were written to missionary churches?

12. What can you say of the morals of the early Christians? How did they worship?

13. Name the officers and leaders of the Apostolic Church. What were their functions?

14. Name five theological tendencies in the Apostolic Age.

CHAPTER II.

From the Apostolic Age to Constantine, 100 to 313 A. D.

I. POLITICS.

The Roman Emperors, from Nerva (96 A. D.) to Marcus Aurelius (161-180), were great statesmen who tried, for the most part, to maintain the dignity and glory of Rome. With Commodus starts a period of decay. Caracalla (211) and Elagabalus were wicked and inhuman to extremes. In 286 Diocletian chose Maximinus associate ruler. The empire had become hopelessly weakened through drunkenness, vice, sensuality, divorce, luxury on the part of the rich and those in authority, and extreme poverty among the masses. The barbarians on the North were breaking through; the Persians on the East revolted.

The statesmen of Rome, realizing the decay of power and the dangers from within and without, often attributed the cause to the decay of the Roman religion and the

31

aggression of Christianity. Through efforts to revive the old Roman religion, Christianity was persecuted.

II. PERSECUTIONS.

The persecutions fall naturally into three periods.

1. From Trajan (98) to Marcus Aurelius (161). These persecutions were not so violent and were of limited area. The Jews revolted under Bar Cochab (132-135), and were suppressed with a loss of 580,000 Jews in Palestine. Many Christians, also, were slain. Polycarp was martyred 155 A. D. The venerable man was urged to revile Christ and save his life, whereupon he answered, " Fourscore and six years I have served him, and he never did me wrong; how then can I revile my King and Savior? " Polycarp was a disciple of John.

2. From Marcus Aurelius to Decius (161-249). These persecutions were more general and were authorized by imperial decrees. Marcus Aurelius (161-180) was a Stoic philosopher, who should have become the first Christian emperor. But he did not understand the Christians, and considered their heroism as mere fanaticism. Earthquakes, famines, and calamities aroused the people against the Christians. In Lyons and Vianna, in Southern Gaul, the Christians were tortured, persecuted and cruelly slain. Justin Martyr was killed in Rome 165 A. D.

3. From Decius to Constantine (249-311). These persecutions were universal, violent, inhuman. Their purpose was to stamp out Christianity. In 248 A. D. was the one thousandth anniversary of the founding of Rome (752 B. C. to 248 A. D.). Rome celebrated this millennium, with a view to regain " Rome's lost glory." To do this, they thought they must revive the ancient religion. Hence Decius made a decree (250) that upon a certain day, over the entire Roman Empire, every person must appear before the magistrates and sacrifice to the gods. Many Christians lapsed and hundreds won the martyr's crown. In 257 Valerian issued an edict, commanding all .Christians to conform to the State religion on pain of banishment. In 258 another edict was issued, more sanguinary than any previous one. Cyprian of Carthage and Sextus of Rome became martyrs at this time. Origen (d. 253) also died from the tortures of persecution. In 303 an edict was everywhere published, commanding that churches be burned, the Scriptures destroyed, and the Christians be degraded and deprived of their freedom. Soon followed another edict, demanding that all Church officials be put in prison and be compelled to sacrifice to the gods. Many Christians delivered up their Scriptures to be burned, to avoid persecution. They were called traditores. In 313 was issued the Edict of Milan, granting religious freedom to the Christians. It also restored the property and civil rights of which they had been deprived.

III. OTHER ENEMIES FROM WITHOUT.

1. Cynicism and Ridicule. Probably during the reign of Marcus Aurelius (170) Celsus wrote a book entitled "True Discourse" (ἀληθὴς λόγος), in which he challenges every vital point in Christianity. His hatred for Jesus knows no bounds. He attempts to reduce all of Christianity to fanaticism and myth. Hardly a single argument has ever been raised against the Christian faith that is not found in Celsus.

2. Lucian (130-200) of Samosata, in Syria, ridiculed and mocked the Christians and their God. In fact, he ridiculed all religion as superstition, but especially directed his mockery and sarcasm against the Christians.

3. Neo-Platonism. Neo-Platonism did not directly oppose Christianity, but tried to supplant it or replace it by an eclectic philosophy. Schaff says, " Neo-Platonism was a direct attempt of the more intelligent and earnest heathenism to rally all its nobler energies, especially the forces of Hellenic philosophy and Oriental mysticism, and to found a universal religion, a pagan counterpart to the Christian." Contemplation and intuition rather than speculation were the way to redemption. It contained magic and divination. Ammonius Saccas (d. 243) was the founder of Neo-Platonism. Plotinus (d. 270) and Porphyry (d. 304) were its greatest advocates. This hostile literature and the persecutions forced the Christians to give reason for their faith, and therefore they wrote the "Apologies," or defenses of Christendom.

IV. ENEMIES OR HERESIES WITHIN THE CHURCH.

1. The Ebionites (meaning of word is " the poor "). Already in Paul's day there were Judaizing Christians, who held that the Gentiles must first become Jews (Epistle to the Galatians). The Ebionites were Jewish Christians who denied the divinity of Christ and held tenaciously to the Mosaic Law. They rejected Paul and held to James and Peter. The earlier Ebionites were Ascetic and exalted virginity. Later ones, in opposition to Gnosticism, married.

2. Gnosticism (knowledge, cf. 1 Tim. 6: 20; 1 Cor. 8: 1). Gnosticism was a speculative philosophy in the Church, which put knowledge (gnosis) above faith. This gnosis was a system of thought, a knowledge of the mysteries which was considered the acme of religion. It may be summed as follows (cf. Moeller, vol. 1, p. 152): (1) Christianity is a practical doctrine of salvation; Gnosticism, a speculative philosophy, a world view, or knowledge of a world-process, for the redemption of the spirit. (2) Gnosticism degrades the Old Testament, holding that Jehovah who created this world (which is evil) is an evil God and not the Supreme Being whom Christ, the Logos, revealed. (3) Christian redemption is victory over the world; Gnosticism is separation of the spirit from matter.

(4) The dualism of experience is transferred from the ethical to the physical realm. Cf. Paul's flesh and spirit, which is purely ethical. (5) Gnosticism explained the creation by the doctrine of emanations or æons which went forth from God. The farthest from God was the most degraded, which was evil enough to create this evil world. This last æon is called a demiurge (Jehovah of Old Testament). (6) The New Testament distinction between spiritual and carnal (pneumatic and hylic) was the same as gnosis and pistis (knowledge and faith). (7) Gnosticism denied the resurrection and the second coming of Jesus. Jesus was "Docetic." (8) The dualism of spirit and sense led either to Asceticism or Libertinism.

3. Manichaeism. This heresy was originated by Mani, in Persia, about 238 A. D. It is a combination of Gnosticism, with a minimum of Christianity, and Zoroastrianism, Old Babylonian philosophies, and other mystic and magical elements. It is based on dualism, the "Kingdom of Light," and the "Kingdom of Darkness." Man is "light imprisoned in darkness." They wholly rejected the Old Testament and explained the remainder in the light of this dualistic philosophy. They had an elaborate organization, and the " elevated priesthood celebrated the secret rites of baptism and communion with solemn pomp, lived as ascetics, possessed no property, and abstained from wine and animal food."

4. Monarchians. The Monarchians denied the doctrine of the Trinity. There were two principal classes of Monarchians. (1) Dynamic—that Jesus was a mere Man, but energized by the Holy Spirit at baptism when he received the divine attributes. This was first proclaimed by Theodotus, 190 A. D., in Rome. Paul of Samosata taught (260) that God is one Person. Jesus was a divinely-begotten Man, not the Logos, Word (John 1: 1 and 6), but raised to dignity and glory by the Logos. (2) Modalistic Monarchianism. Sabellius is the most famous teacher of this doctrine. God the Father is the Source or Energy of all. The Son is the Father as Redeemer or Savior; the Holy Spirit is the Father giving holiness to men. Hence the Son and Holy Spirit are only modes or activities of the one God.

V. REFORM MOVEMENTS WITHIN THE CHURCH.

The following were Puritanic and Reformatory:

1. Montanism. Montanus, with several women, Priscilla and Maximilla, from Pepuza, Phrygia, claimed to have received new revelations from the Paraclete (Holy Spirit). See John 14:16, 26; 15:26. These Montanists, believing they had the Paraclete, were not bound by the Scriptures. They tried to purify the Church, hence were very rigorous and legalistic. They distinguished between mortal sins, which the Church could not forgive, and venial sins, which could be forgiven. Of the former, they held the following: homicide, idolatry, fraud, denial of the faith, blasphemy, adultery and fornication. They were ascetic and expected the speedy end of the world.

2. Novatianism. This was legalistic Montanism striving to purify the Church by discipline. During the Decian persecution (250 A. D.) many Christians lapsed. After the persecutions, many of these came back into the Church. There were two parties: (1) Those who were lenient and accepted them easily and readily, and (2) the followers of Novatian, who demanded rebaptism for readmission into the Church. These Novatians believed in baptismal regeneration and demanded that baptism be administered by the proper person. They separated from the Church and continued for awhile.

3. **Donatism.** During the persecutions of 303-305 many Christians gave up their Scriptures to be burned to avoid suffering. These traditores also asked admission into the Church after the Edict of Milan (311) forever put an end to persecutions. Donatus of North Africa was the leader of the opposition demanding the Novatian principle of rebaptism by a proper person, and also holding that no man can hold office who lapsed during the persecutions. The Donatists appealed to Constantine in their troubles, but he decided against them. Hereafter they strongly urged the doctrine of the separation of the Church and State. These Donatists became legalistic reactionaries and retarded rather than furthered the cause of Christ.

VI. LITERATURE.

1. **Literature for Edification.** These are utterances, epistles and writings by the

apostolic fathers, which show us the piety and faith of their day.

(1) First Epistle of Clement to the Church at Corinth. Clement was bishop at Rome and wrote this epistle between 93 and 97 A. D. Clement gives wholesome advice to the Corinthian Church, how to settle their difficulties, and admonishes them to humility. He quotes freely from the Old Testament, which is the Scriptures of the Christians.

(2) Epistle of Barnabas. This is not the Barnabas who labored with Paul. The most probable date is 130-131 A. D. (Harnack.) This epistle uses the Old Testament allegorically to prove the truths of Christianity, as against the Jews, who reject Christianity because they never understood their own revelation, i. e., the Old Testament.

(3) The Epistles of Ignatius. Ignatius was Bishop of Antioch, had been a pupil of John, and was torn to pieces by the lions at Rome December 20, to amuse the Romans. The year is not known, either 107 A. D. or 115 A. D. Ignatius in his epistles exhorts the churches to be obedient to their bishops and presbyters. He wrote letters to the Ephesians, Magnesians, Trallians,

Romans, Philadelphians, Smyrnaeans, and to Polycarp.

(4) The Shepherd of Hermas. Hermas was a pastor of the Roman Church about 129-140 A. D. His book is divided into three parts: (a) Five Visions, (b) Twelve Commands, (c) Ten Similitudes. It was widely read and is sometimes called "The Pilgrim's Progress" of the Early Church.

(5) Polycarp's Epistle to the Philippians. Polycarp was Bishop of Smyrna, and suffered martyrdom Feb. 23, 155 A. D. Polycarp in this epistle strengthens the faith of the Philippians by directing them to the gospel literature.

(6) The Didache (the Teaching of the Twelve Apostles). This is generally believed to have been written after the Apostolic Age, 100-150 A. D. The first part of the Didache treats of the "Two Ways," which was instructions to converts before baptism. The second part treats of baptism, fasts, Lord's supper, and the officers of the Church. It closes with an exhortation in which the "Second Coming" is referred to.

2. The Apologetic Period. The persecutions brought forth defenses or apologies on the part of the Christians. The apologists are Quadratus, Aristides, Justin, Tatian, Athenagoras, Theophilus, Hermias and Melito. These apologies were written, not to compel others to accept Christianity, but to convince them that Christianity had a right to exist. The most important of these apologies were addressed to the Emperors Antonius Pius and Marcus Aurelius. The Christians were charged with atheism, licentiousness, and cannibalism; atheism, because the Christians rejected the Roman gods and the heathen could not conceive of the Christian's God as Spirit. The charge of licentiousness was due to the fact that the Christians met at night for worship, and because they manifested strong brotherly affections for each other. The apologists show that for the Christians even a licentious thought is sin. Cannibalism grew out of the eucharist, wherein the Christians symbolically partook of the body and blood of Christ. The apologists again showed that for the Christians, murder was the most heinous of sins.

Furthermore, the apologists showed that Christianity was not a new religion, but the oldest in the world. Moses wrote the Pentateuch, says Justin, before the Trojan War. They draw most of their arguments from prophecy and fulfillment, miracles, and the transforming power of the Gospel of Christ. Justin, the Martyr, was the greatest apologist.

3. Polemical Literature. Heresies within the Church (see §§ IV and V) brought forth polemics. Their purpose was to defeat and correct the errors that were rapidly spreading within the Church. Now the New Testament is quoted as authority. The apologists used the Old Testament. Since "authority" is demanded to meet these errors, the idea, for the first time, of an orthodox Catholic Church, comes to view.

(1) Irenæus (b. 130-135 A. D.) of Asia Minor, a pupil of Polycarp, and well educated in the classics, was one of the ablest writers against "Heresies." He became pastor at Lyons, France (177). About the year 185 he wrote his "Five Books Against Heresies."

(2) Hippolytus flourished about 222-235 at Rome. He wrote "Reputation of All Heresies."

(3) Tertullian (b. 150-160) was a native of Carthage, North Africa. He was a well-

44

educated lawyer, and the founder of Latin theology. Tertullian was a voluminous writer, and not only wrote against all kinds of heresies, but upon nearly every subject in theology. He died about 220 A. D.

(4) Cyprian (b. 200) suffered martyrdom (258) under Valerian. Cyprian did most to create and develop the doctrine of the Catholic Church.

(5) Theological Literature (Alexandrian School). Alexandria was the seat of speculative philosophy, and here first was the attempt made to make a " systematic exposition of Christianity as a whole." The allegorical method of interpreting Scriptures was reduced to a system.

(6) Clement of Alexandria (b. 160) was probably born at Athens. He succeeded Pantaenus as teacher of the Catechetical School at Alexandria about 190 A. D., and continued till 202, when persecution drove him away. Clement was profoundly speculative and brought the Greek philosophy to Christian thought.

(7) Origen. Born about 185, of Christian parents, was unusually pious, lived an ascetic life and was with difficulty restrained from offering himself as a martyr in 202,

when his father, Leonides, suffered that
fate. In 203 Origen became teacher of the
catechetical school. He was a great student
of philosophy and leaned heavily toward
gnosticism, but was stayed by the historical
foundations of Christianity. He was tortured during the Decian persecution, and
died 258. His writings are on: (a) Critical,
Exegetical, and Edificatory Works on the
Bible. (b) Apologetics. (c) Dogmatics.
(d) Practical Works. (e) Theology. (f)
Concerning God. (g) The Son. (h) Holy
Spirit. (i) Anthropology. (j) Baptism.
(k) Eschatology.

VII. THE CANON.

The heresies within the Church, especially gnosticism, forced the Christians to a rule
(canon) of authority. Hence they sought
for the true writings of the apostles. A
great flood of literature was read in the
churches, which was attributed to the apostles. The process of determining which are
the true and worthy books lasted from
about 140 A. D. to 395 A. D., although by
the end of our period (313) the canon was
practically determined.

VIII. THE RISE OF THE CATHOLIC CHURCH.

1. Dogma. (1) At first religion was an inner experience—Christ in the heart. It was personal,—the theology of the Good Shepherd. (2) As the Church entered Greek and Roman territory and became prevailingly Gentile, in conflict with heathenism, religion becomes more and more a matter of creeds, statements and definitions of truth. Where the real experience lacked, men sought authority in creeds and definitions. (3) The next development was a basis for the second grade, demanding an "authoritative channel" for the truth. Hence the Church and bishops guaranteed the authority of the religious life. This change, making the authority external instead of inner experience, is the essence of the Roman Church.

2. Centralization. During the Apostolic Age presbyters (elders) and bishops were of equal rank, or were the same persons. Furthermore, there were several or many of these in each local church. Now the bishop is one and exercises authority over all the others. This change was furthered by (1) following the example of the Roman Government, which was a model of perfection to all Gentile converts, and (2) the need for organization and concentration through persecutions and missionary endeavors. This developed the pope.

IX. CHURCH EXTENSION.

" The Christians numbered 500 in 30 A. D., grew to 500,000 by 100 A. D., and increased to 30,000,000 by 311 A. D." (Flick, " The Rise of the Mediæval Church," p. 54.) Christianity (313) extended from Britain to India and Mesopotamia. Christians abounded in all the countries and cities bordering the Mediterranean. It began with a few poor peasants, and now counted among its numbers the educated, the influential and finally the Roman Emperor, Constantine. " In general, we may characterize the present period as the period of the gradual growth and the gradual corruption of Christianity until it became strong enough, on the one hand, to make its adoption by the empire a matter of policy, and corrupt enough, on the other, to rejoice in such adoption." (Newman, vol. 1, page 148.)

X. CHRISTIAN LIFE AND WORSHIP.

To do justice to the Christians, their morals should be compared with the pagan life from which they came. Language can hardly express the vice, superstition, degradation, slavery, hopelessness, and general wickedness of the pagans. The Christians, in contrast, sanctified the home, lived chaste lives, pledged themselves not to steal, kill, nor harm others, and they were hopeful and optimistic in facing calamities and death.

However, the pagans coming into the Church in large numbers, could not be quickly or completely reformed. They brought with them into the Church much of their heathen superstition, their vices and views of life. Worship became more ritualistic. Sacerdotalism took the place of spirituality. The priest displaced the prophet; formalism prevailed instead of morality; and the ordinances were supposed to have magical powers for the propitiation of God, rather than symbols for man to repent.

Baptism was mostly by triune immersion in running water, for believers only, but infant baptism crept in through this magical idea of the rite. The Didache (130) speaks thus of Baptism: " Now concerning baptism, baptize in the following manner: Having said all these things before [the instructions] baptize into the name of the Father, and of the Son, and of the Holy Ghost in living [running] water. But if you do not have living water baptize into other water; and if you are not able to baptize in cold [baptize], in warm. But if you have neither, then pour upon the head water three times into the name of Father, and Son, and Holy Spirit." (Translation my own.)

The agape (love feast) was held with and sometimes separate from the " Lord's supper " (bread and wine). Many abuses crept in.

Church festivals increased in number and retained much of the heathen element. Easter and Christmas became important days; so also Pentecost. Sunday instead of Sabbath was the day of worship.

The symbolism of the catacombs shows the better side of the triumphant faith and hope of the true Church of Christ.

QUESTIONS.

1. What was the character of the Roman emperors of this period? Of Roman society?
2. Name the three periods of persecution. What were some of the causes of persecution? Name several prominent martyrs. What was the Edict of Milan?

QUESTIONS

3. Who was Celsus? Lucian? How did Neo-Platonism hinder Christianity?

4. Which is the worse, enemies without, or within the Church? Name the heresies of the Church. Who were the Ebionites? Name three points of Gnosticism. Where did Manichaism come from? Describe Sabellianism.

5. Name the reform movements in the Church. Can the Church be reformed by discipline from without?

6. Name the four kinds of literature of this period. Describe each kind. Name two writers of each period.

7. What is the canon? When was it completed? What causes led the Church to select some and reject other books for the rule of faith?

8. Name several causes that led to the formation of a highly-organized Church.

9. Describe the growth of Christendom. What was the result of this phenomenal growth?

10. How did the morals of the Christians compare with the heathen? What effect did the heathen converts have upon the Church? How did this heathenism affect the worship of the Church?

CHAPTER III.

From Constantine to Gregory I. 313 to 590 A. D.

I. POLITICS.

1. In 312 A. D. **Constantine** gained his victory over Maxentius. Before the battle, it is said, he saw a vision of the cross or the Labarum with the words, " In this conquer." He promised the Lord to become a Christian if he conquered. In 313 he, with his associate, Licinus, his brother-in-law, issued the Edict of Milan, which gave Christianity a legal right to exist, and also restored to the Christians their confiscated property. In 323 Constantine gained a victory over Licinus and thereby became sole ruler.

Constantine was a converted heathen, and emperor over pagans as well as Christians. His life does not come up to the Christian standard; nevertheless his sympathies were Christian, which is best shown in the changed laws.

" He abolished the punishment of crucifixion. He exerted himself to prevent the practice of exposing or murdering newborn infants. His laws against unchastity were very strict. In 316 he forbade the practice of branding criminals on their face. In 320 the laws against celibacy, enacted to promote the Roman birth rate, were relaxed to favor the Christians, who wished to live an ascetic life. In 321 all legal business was forbidden on Sundays. The bishops were allowed important legal prerogatives and to hold their own courts, and their decisions were ratified by a positive law." (Pullan, " The Church of the Fathers," p. 230.)

2. Constantine Made his Capital of the empire at Byzantium (326), which now became Constantinople. This left the Bishop of Rome the most important official in the Eternal City, and promoted the primacy of Rome that ultimately developed into the papacy.

3. During This Period we have the Barbarian invasions. The Roman Empire was weakened by centuries of vice and luxury, while the Barbarians to the north grew stronger and more oppressive. The Huns were driving the Goths, and now these

Teutons crossed the Danube and entered Italy. Alaric invaded Greece and was defeated 402-403 A. D. In 406 an army of from 200,000 to 400,000 of these German tribes was defeated by Stilicho near Florence. In 409 Alaric came to Rome and was paid a ransom. In 410 a larger army under Alaric entered Rome and sacked the city, but spared the lives of the people and Christian temples. In 451 Attila, the Hun, was defeated at Chalons (France). In 452 he threatened Rome, and was pacified by the Roman bishop and his embassy. In 455 the Vandals sacked Rome. They had already plundered North Africa.

4. **Fall of the Roman Empire in the West (476).** From the year 395 on there were two emperors, one in the East (Constantinople) and one in the West (Rome). In 475 Romulus Augustulus, a child of six, became emperor at Rome. Odoacer, leader of a tribe of Germans, dethroned him and became " Patrician " of Italy. Zeno, at Constantinople was emperor alone, and henceforth there was but one emperor until the restoration of the West under Charles the Great, 800 A. D. Again the Roman bishop was the most important personage at Rome for hundreds of years.

II. CHURCH AND STATE.

The Church and State became one. The emperor freed and defended the Church and therefore claimed the right to rule it. The bishops, for a long time held in special honor, became more haughty since the Church came into universal favor and power. "But whatever respect the emperors might pay to the Church and its officers, they had in fact immense influence over it from the time when the emperors became Christians, says Socrates. The affairs of the Church depended upon them. It could hardly be otherwise. Privileges were conferred by law upon the Catholic Church alone, and occasions unfortunately soon arose when it was necessary for the emperor to say which of two contending parties he considered Catholic. If the defeated party asked what the emperor had to do with the Church, the victors replied, that the Church was in the State and that none was over the emperor but God. The fathers at Constantinople, in the year 448, when an imperial rescript had been read, cried out, 'Long live our high priest the emperor.' Edicts issued by the emperor were published in the churches. And as the emperor, by influence or direct nomination, secured the election of many bishops, especially of those of Constantinople, the Episcopal order was generally disposed to do him homage. Justinian showed much favor to the Church, but at the same time he made it more directly subject to the State." (Cheetham, "Church History, Early Period," p. 173.)

III. THEOLOGY AND THEOLOGIANS.

"We find everywhere two great principles of human nature in perpetual conflict. On the one hand, respect for authority, dread of change, desire to maintain the state of things in which each man finds himself. On the other, more reliance on the powers which God has given man, more hopefulness, more readiness to leave the things which are behind and to press forward to those which are before. To speak generally, we may say that the Latin Church took the conservative side, the Greek that of free discussion and inquiry." (Cheetham, p. 215.) This difference in human nature produces schools of thought. We have in this period the schools of Antioch, Alexandria and the West.

CONSTANTINE TO GREGORY I.

1. Antioch. The theologians of Antioch insisted upon the necessity of grammatical and historical exposition of the Scriptures. John Chrysostom (347-407) was probably the greatest of this school. Also Eusebius of Emesa, Cyril of Jerusalem (350-386), Theodore of Mopsuestia (393-428), and Theodoret (390-457).

2. Alexandria. The Alexandrian school was speculative rather than exegetical. In the theological controversies of this period the Alexandrians emphasized the divinity of Christ more than his humanity, while the Antiochenes held firmly to his humanity. The important men of this school were Eusebius of Cæsarea (270-341), the father of Church history; Athanasius (246-373), the champion of orthodoxy against Arius; Epiphanius (315-403), the three Cappadocians, Basil (330-379), Gregory Nazianzen (325-389) and Gregory of Nyssa (335-395).

3. The West. The theologians of the West were supremely practical, interested in church organization, missions, and getting things done. "The spirit of the old empire passed into the Latin Church." The Great Men of the West were Hilary of Poitiers (320-366), Ambrose (340-397), Jerome

(346-420), Rufinus (345-410), and Augustine (354-430). (Moncrief, p. 124.)

IV. DOCTRINAL CONTROVERSIES.

The Trinity; Arius. Constantine had scarcely legalized the Church until he found it torn by factions. First the Donatists in Africa, then the Arian controversy. Arius was a presbyter at Alexandria who held heretical views. He said: (1) The Son is a creation out of nothing by the will of God the Father. (2) A Divine Being, created before the worlds, but still a creature. (3) As a father must exist before his Son, so the Son of God is not coeternal with the Father. (4) There was, when he (the Son) was not. (5) It was through him that God made the world. (6) Yet he is not in his proper nature incapable of sin. (7) However, by exertion of his own will, he was preserved from it. (Cheetham, p. 256.)

Bishop Alexander of Alexandria asserted the coexistence of God the Father and God the Son from all eternity. There never was a time when God was not Father, and the Son was not the Son. Arius thought Alexander was a Sabellian, and he wanted to preserve the Trinity, but really destroyed the Trinity by making Christ neither divine nor human. Constantine sent Hosius with a letter to Alexandria, asking them to settle the dispute, but without avail. The emperor then called the Council of Nicæa (see description of this council in Stanley, Eastern Church), 325 A. D., where 318 bishops assembled to decide the dispute. The emperor himself presided over the council. Athenasius of Alexandria was the opponent of Arius and the victor at the council. The following creed was adopted: " We believe in one God, the Father Almighty, Maker of all things visible and invisible, and in one Lord Jesus Christ, the Son of God, begotten of the Father, the only-begotten; that is of the essence of the Father, God of God, Light of Light, very God of very God, begotten, not made, being of one substance (Homoousios) with the Father; by whom all things were made, both in heaven and on earth; who for us men, and for our salvation, came down and was incarnate and was made man; he suffered and the third day he rose again, ascended into heaven; from thence he shall come to judge the quick and the dead. And in the Holy Ghost."

" But those who say ' There was a time when he was not '; and ' He was not before he was made '; and ' He was made out of nothing,' or ' He is of another substance or essence,' or ' The Son of God is created,' or ' changeable,' or ' alterable,'—they are condemned by the holy Catholic and Apostolic Church." (Schaff's " Creeds of Christendom," vol. I, p. 28f.)

V. DOCTRINAL CONTROVERSIES— CHRISTOLOGY.

The Council of Nicæa settled the doctrine of the Trinity, and also declared the perfect divinity and perfect humanity of Christ. From now on the problem is, how are these two natures combined?—the problem of Christology.

1. Apollinarius, Bishop of Laodicea, explained the problem in this way: Man is body, soul and spirit. The Logos (Word, John 1: 14) took the place of the " Spirit " in man. The Council of Constantinople (381) condemned his views and reasserted and extended the Nicene Creed.

2. Nestorius, Bishop of Constantinople, objected to the word " Theotokos," " mother of God," referring to Mary, in the confessions of the day. Nestorius held that Mary was not the " mother of God," but Christotokos, " mother of Christ." A council at

Ephesus (431) condemned Nestorius. Cyril of Alexandria was the champion of this council.

3. Eutyches, Abbot of Constantinople, in 448 put forth the theory that Christ had only one nature. That is, the human nature was absorbed by the Divine, as a drop of honey would be absorbed by the ocean. A council of Eutychians met at Ephesus in 449, where they carried the day by chicanery and force. The bishops fought with fists and clubs. The Bishop of Constantinople was killed. The Œcumenical Council of Chalcedon (451) condemned Eutychianism and adopted the Chalcedonian Creed.

4. Monophysitism (one nature). Immediately after the Council of Chalcedon, the one-nature idea continued. It now took a slightly different form. Eutyches said that the human nature was absorbed by the divine. The theory now is that the two natures were fused together into a new nature—a tertium quid, a third thing. "He was **of** two natures; he was not **in** two natures." This heresy denied both his humanity and divinity. The second Council of Constantinople (553) condemned Monophysitism.

VI. DOCTRINAL CONTROVERSIES—ANTHROPOLOGY.

The Pelagian Controversy. Augustine, the greatest of the Church fathers (354-430), had a remarkable conversion from a life of sin. His own experience, naturally, colored his theology. He taught, "Man freely fell in Adam, and in the fall lost his ability, and was utterly undone—became a mass of perdition; he is saved by grace alone, without any coöperation on his own part; through grace his freedom is restored, and again he is in harmony with the Spirit of God; but God, for good and sufficient reasons, willed to save some but not all of the fallen race; salvation outside the visible Church is impossible." (Moncrief, p. 143.)

Pelagius, on the other hand, had no remarkable conversion, did not feel the total depravity and helplessness of man, and emphasized free will. "In the system of Pelagius men were made mortal. They did not become such by Adam's sin. As far as they are sinners it is by doing as Adam did. All good or evil is something done by us, for we are capable of either. There is at our birth nothing within us but what God placed there. The supposition of sin in infants before the exercise of reason, prior to the 'election' [choice] of evil, is monstrous." (Fisher, "History of Doctrine," p. 190.) This Augustine-Pelagian controversy has continued through the centuries, and has affected all classes in the Church.

VII. CHURCH EXTENSION.

1. **Ulfilas,** born of Greek and Gothic parents (311), was taught Arian Christianity, made bishop 341 by Eusebius, and worked among the Goths till his death in 383. He was called the "Moses" of his people. Largely through his labors all the Germanic tribes became Arian Christians. His great work was the translation of the Bible into Gothic, having invented a Gothic alphabet for the purpose.

2. **Conversion of the Franks.** In 496 Clovis, King of the Franks, was converted to Catholic Christianity. His whole army was baptized also by immersion. In 589 Recarred, King of the Visigoths of Spain, also became a Catholic.

3. **St. Martin of Tours** (d. 397), the soldier-bishop, worked mostly in central France and won crowds of converts.

4. **St. Patrick,** born about 400 A. D., was a Briton. He was captured by pirates and

taken to Ireland, where he served seven years as a slave. Having escaped he went to Gaul, where he was made a presbyter and bishop. He returned to Ireland, and by his persuasive personality, his executive ability and missionary zeal, converted Ireland to Christianity, and founded the first Christian school at Armagh.

5. Columba (b. 521) was born in Ireland, expelled, then went as missionary among the Picts of Scotland, where he did a great work.

6. Columban, born (543) in Bangor, Ireland, did splendid missionary work in Burgundy, Switzerland, and Northern Italy. He was one of the most capable men of his day.

VIII. CHRISTIAN LIFE AND WORSHIP.

The Church was growing in power, but losing in spirituality. The Christian emperors, indeed, made better laws, and enforced many reformations. But when virtue is enforced by law it ceases to be virtue, but mere formal conduct. The Sunday was established by law, and became a festival; Christianity was made popular, and hordes of unregenerate pagans entered the Church;

65

Church union destroyed freedom of thought; favors to the bishops made them proud and worldly.

Christianity was secularized, and became extremely worldly and corrupt. The pagans worshiped many gods; now they worship the saints and martyrs. Formerly they worshiped idols; now they worship images. Once the pagans persecuted the Christians; now as Christians they persecute the pagans and one another. As pagans they sacrificed to propitiate the angry gods; now they use the symbols (baptism, Lord's supper, etc.) as magical sacraments to propitiate God. Religion became formal, sacerdotal, ecclesiastical.

Many noble souls, who studied their Bibles and drank from the pure Fountain of Life and Light, revolted against the worldliness and corruption of the Church. The revolt took the form of escape from the world rather than attempting to transform conditions. Monasticism is the form in which individualism and piety expressed themselves.

IX. MONASTICISM.

Asceticism is nowhere taught in the New Testament. The contrast between flesh and spirit in Paul is ethical and not physical. But Gnosticism and Manichæism taught that matter as such is evil. Hence the idea that mortifying the flesh and enduring physical agonies would be meritorious came to be generally believed. The increase of worldliness in the Church brought about the opposite extreme—to escape from the world. The Ascetics spent their time in fastings and prayer, remained celibate, and lived lives of self-torture and austerities. Asceticism began to take various forms.

1. The Anchorite was a hermit who withdrew by himself to some desert place and lived an ascetic life. Anthony, born about 351, lived in a cleft in a rock. From here he secluded himself yet more, where he remained twenty years. His fame spread and again he withdrew from men. "Anthony's food was bread and salt, which he never tasted until after sunset. He often fasted entirely for two or three days. He watched and prayed all night, sleeping only a little time on the ground." (Jerome.)

2. The Cœnobites were hermits who lived together. Usually a hermit who attained fame for his austerities was surrounded by younger hermits, who imitated him. This is the beginning of cloister life. Both the Anchorites and Cœnobites originated in Egypt, where the climate favored this life. Pachomius organized a society of monks on an island in the Nile which, during his lifetime, reached 3,000 in number. By 400 his monks numbered 50,000. Their ascetic practices may be divided into four classes: dietetic, sexual, social and spiritual. Fastings, celibacy or continency, withdrawal from the world, and hundreds of prayers daily, characterize the early hermit monks.

3. **Western Monasticism.** Benedict of Nursia (480-543). All the great leaders and fathers of the Church favored monasticism. Jerome, Athanasius, Augustine, Basil and others promoted it. "Western monasticism was a more practical system, an economic factor, a powerful missionary machine, an educational agency, and the pioneer of civilization." (Flick, p. 212.) Benedict of Nursia was the great organizer and unifier of Western monasticism. "He became a severe Ascetic, wore a hair shirt, and a monk's dress of skins, rolled in beds of thistles to subdue the flesh, and chose to be ignorant and holy rather than to be educated and wicked." He founded the monastery

at Monte Casino, near Naples, which he organized so perfectly that it became the model for all Europe. He established the "rule" of obedience: labor, chastity, and poverty.

"At one time the Benedictines had 37,-000 monasteries, and altogether produced twenty-four popes, 200 cardinals, 4,000 bishops, and 55,505 saints." (Flick, p. 216.)

"In favor of monasticism it may be said (1) that it made strong resistance to worldliness; (2) it was a powerful means of attracting pagans to Christianity; (3) in many instances, it promoted theological study; (4) it afforded a refuge and means of reformation for those that were cast out from society."

Furthermore, the monasteries kept up some of the ordinances and practices of the apostles, which the Church in general had neglected. Especially feet-washing. (See Hastings, "Encyclopedia of Religion and Ethics," art. feet-washing.)

"On the other hand, (1) monasticism withdrew large numbers of good men from active service in Christ's cause; (2) it fostered spiritual pride and hypocrisy; (3) it filled Christendom with radically wrong ideas of religion and morality; (4) it brutalized many men; (5) it was the most influential factor in the development of hierarchy." (Newman, vol. 1, p. 319.)

QUESTIONS.

1. Name four political events of this period. Did these events affect the Church? How?

2. What influences for good and evil did the union of Church and State have upon Christianity?

3. What are the characteristics of each of the three schools of theologians? Name two of each school.

4. What was the Arian controversy about? What did Arius believe? When was the Council of Nicæa? What was the result of the council?

5. What is the problem of Christology? Name the four great councils that dealt with this problem. What heresy was condemned at each?

6. What was Augustine's teaching about man? Pelagius'? Which do you hold?

7. Name the great missionaries of this period. What special work did Ulfilas do? St. Patrick?

8. What effect did wealth and power have upon the Church? How did the hordes of pagan Christians affect the worship?

9. What is Asceticism? An Anchorite? The Cœnobites? Who organized western monasticism? Describe the growth of monasticism. Name three favorable and three unfavorable criticisms of monasticism.

CHAPTER IV.

From Gregory to Charlemagne
590 to 814 A. D.

I. POLITICS.

Rome fell in 476. The Roman Emperor resided at Constantinople. Clovis, King of the Franks, died 511. The successors of Clovis seemed to lose in power while their major-domos increased in authority and dignity. The Carolingian line came from these majors. Charles Martel defeated the Mohammedans at Poictiers, in 732. This was one of the decisive battles of the world. His son Pepin aided the pope against the Lombards, who came into Italy (568) and took possession of the territory adjacent to Rome and also threatened the city. Having defeated the Lombards Pepin gave the land to the pope (752-757). Childeric III. was the nominal king and Pepin the major, but the latter succeeded in sending the former to a monastery and had himself anointed king by Archbishop Boniface

(752), and later by the pope (753). Pepin died (768) and was succeeded by Karl or Charles the Great (Charlemagne), who reigned from 768 to 814.

Charlemagne was one of the greatest men in history. He conquered, combined, and developed the Germanic tribes and forged anew the Roman Empire of the West. He also aided the pope against the Lombards and confirmed the gift of Pepin. At Christmas, in 800, while Charlemagne was kneeling in St. Peter's Church at Rome, Pope Leo III. placed the crown upon his head, as Emperor of the Roman Empire. The Emperor in the East was too weak to resist, and steadily declined until the fall of Constantinople (1453).

II. CHURCH AND STATE.

The gift of Pepin to the pope, and the pope's crowning of Charlemagne, are the source of endless troubles and discussions. It is the question of the primacy of the pope over secular affairs. How it was understood in that day can easily be seen from Charlemagne's conduct.

The emperor appointed the bishops and primates of the Church, called councils, and conducted not only the affairs of State, but Church also.

The pope, being a landowner, soon imagined that he owned the earth, and that all kings and rulers were his subjects in temporal things as well as spiritual. The false decretals have a fabrication, stating that Constantine gave Italy to the pope. This falsehood was invented to back up the papal claims.

During the reign of Charlemagne the emperor was supreme in civil and religious matters.

III. GREGORY THE GREAT (590-604).

Gregory was a monk of great piety and zeal. He was literally forced to become Bishop (pope) of Rome. A great man was needed because the political and ecclesiastical conditions were in a most demoralizing condition. Gregory's genius turned the trend of affairs, which makes his reign the beginning of a new epoch.

1. As Administrator of the see of Rome Gregory elevated the priesthood, purified the Church, and spiritualized religion. Religion in the sixth century was at a low ebb, and Gregory did much to better conditions.

2. As Patriarch of the West he managed the religious life in Italy, Gaul, Spain, Africa and Britain. He promoted great missionary activities, and unified and systematized the Church.

3. As Temporal Ruler, Gregory, by force of necessity, directed the civil affairs of Rome, saved the city from the Lombards, made a treaty of peace with them and finally brought about their conversion. The Roman Emperor Maurice resided at Constantinople, and the Exarch at Ravenna neglected Rome, which was constantly harassed by the Lombards, who came into Italy in 567.

IV. CHURCH EXTENSION— MISSIONS.

1. England. The Gospel was carried to England very early and an independent Church grew up there. In 596 Gregory sent his friend Augustine, with forty companions, to Britain. They were well received by King Ethelbert, whose queen, Bertha, was a Catholic. The Catholic faith increased until the Council of Whitby (664), when the whole Anglo-Saxon Church in Britain became Catholic. The Venerable Bede (672-735) was one of the best fruits of England missions, and one of the ablest scholars of his day.

74

2. Germany. Columbanus, the Irish monk, labored in Burgundy and Switzerland (590-615). Gallus, the founder of the monastery of St. Gall, in Switzerland, a coworker with Columbanus, did most to convert the Swiss and Swabians (590-640). The great missionary to the Germans was Boniface (Winfried) (680-755), from Devonshire, England, the apostle to Thuringia. He also labored among the Hessians, Saxons, and Bavarians. He made several journeys to Rome (719, 723), whereupon he was made missionary bishop, through which he brought all Germany under the pope. Boniface died a martyr in Friesland in 755, at the age of 75.

3. Holland. Willibrord (692-741), another Englishman, labored in Friesland, where he became Bishop of Utrecht. He, also, was a warm supporter of Rome, and a friend to Boniface.

4. Eastern Asia. "Timotheus, who was the Nestorian Patriarch from 778 to 820, may be mentioned as the warmest advocate of missions. He sent out a large band of monks from the convent of Beth-abe, in Mesopotamia, to evangelize the Tartar tribes, who roved in the neighborhood of

the Caspian Sea; and some of them pene-
trated as far as India and China, either
planting or reviving in those distant parts
a knowledge of the Gospel." (Hardwick,
" Middle Age," p. 27.)

V. MOHAMMEDANISM.

Mohammed (570-632), the founder of a
new religion, caused the greatest hindrance
and menace to Christianity. As a boy, he
was subject to epilepsy, and as he grew up,
to visions and dreams. He spent much time
in solitude and meditation. Out of a mixture
of perverted Christianity, Judaism and Ara-
bian idolatry and mysticism, he founded a
synchretistic religion (the Koran), completely rejecting idolatry, and proclaiming
God as one God whose character is power
and will. Mohammedanism tends toward
fatalism, holds a low ideal of woman, sanc-
tions polygamy, and its idea of heaven is
licensed sensuality.

In 611 Mohammed proclaimed his religion
at Mecca, but without much success. In
622 he fled to Medina (the Hegira), where
he became master. He returned with the
power of the sword and took Mecca (630).
He issued an edict that all idolaters should

be killed unless they were converted to his faith. At his death (632) nearly all Arabia was conquered. In 637 Omar, the second caliph, took Jerusalem, and was master of Syria (639). Egypt was added (640), Persia (651), North Africa (707), it (Mohammedanism) was established in Spain (711), crossed the Pyrenees and was checked by Charles Martel (732) at Tours. "The defenseless patriarchates of Jerusalem, of Antioch, and Alexandria, deprived of their rightful pastors, and curtailed on every side, are moving illustrations of the general ruin; and out of four hundred sees that once shed a salutary light on Africa, four only were surviving in the eleventh century. The rest had been absorbed into the vortex of Islamism." (Hardwick, p. 33.)

Had Mohammedanism ever arisen, or spread, if the Church of the East had been more missionary and her life more pure? Today, Islam is the one rival of Christianity to become a world religion.

VI. THE FIRST POPE, HADRIAN I.

At the Council of Chalcedon (451) five patriarchates were established—Jerusalem, Antioch, Alexandria, Constantinople and Rome. All of these were equal in authority. How then did the bishop at Rome become a pope?

1. Rome Was an Apostolic See—presided over by the Apostle Peter as the first bishop (according to tradition only).

2. Rome Was for Years the imperial city, the capital of the world, and hence the bishop at Rome was honored with the city.

3. The Church at Rome was stronger than the others, more aggressive, more missionary.

4. The Spirit of the West was practical, not speculative. The same spirit that made Rome great, politically, also made the Church at Rome aggressive and dominating.

5. The Removal of the Capital to Constantinople left the Roman bishop the most important personage in the Eternal City. In the times of danger and crisis the bishop saved the city. In 452 Leo I. pacified Attila the Hun.

6. The Greatness of Gregory in managing Church and civic affairs elevated the Roman bishop above others.

7. The Immense Territory of the West, all under one patriarch, the Bishop of Rome, and the extensive missionary activities un-

der his direction, gave him a virtual supremacy over the Catholic Church.

**8. The Weakness of the Eastern
Churches,** and their overthrow by Mohammedanism, left the Roman bishop the actual
head, and finally the theoretical head of the
entire Church.

9. Hadrian I. (772-795) was the first pope
who claimed that the seat of Peter (the
bishop at Rome) was bishop of the universal Church (sedes apostolica caput totius
mundi et omnium Dei ecclesiarum).

10. Furthermore, during the doctrinal
controversies of the Church, Rome was, for
the most part, orthodox. This, too, gave
Rome a preëminence.

VII. DOCTRINAL CONTROVERSIES.

1. The Adoptionist Controversy. In the
last chapter we discussed the Christological
controversies. One more claims our attention. Elipandus, of Toledo, Spain, was pro-
moter of the theory that Christ was the
Son of God only on the divine side, and on
the human side he was adopted as the Son.
This theory denied the incarnation. It was
condemned at a number of councils—Ratis-

bon 792, Frankfort 794, Aachen 799, and Rome 800.

2. The Filioque Controversy. In the West the creeds stated that the Holy Spirit proceeded from the "Father and the Son" (filioque), while in the East the confessions had only "the Father." At the Council of Toledo (589) the "filioque" was added to the creeds of Nicæa and Constantinople.

3. Iconoclastic Controversy. The Church was composed almost entirely of heathen converts who formerly worshiped idols. After they became Christians they had images (eikōns) in the churches. The Jews and Mohammedans ridiculed the Christians for their idolatry. In 726 Emperor Leo issued an edict, forbidding the kneeling before images and pictures. A second edict (730) doomed images to destruction, the cross alone excepted. The second Council of Nicæa decided that "bowing and honorable adoration should be offered to all sacred images; but this external and inferior worship must not be confounded with the true and supreme worship which belongs exclusively to God."

4. The Paulicians. In the seventh century, in Armenia, a sect arose who rejected the Old Testament, and most of the New Testament except Paul (hence the name). They rejected all forms and ordinances. They were absolute dualists, and largely gnostic in belief. Their conception of Christ was docetic.

VIII. CULTURE AND SCHOOLS.

Charlemagne gathered around him the greatest scholars of his age. Alcuin of England became his "intellectual prime minister." Peter of Pisa, and Paul the Deacon, and others were also called to his court. The clergy were ignorant; therefore he provided for their education. He founded schools at Paris, Tours, Corbie, Orleans, Lyons, Toulouse, Clugny, Mainz, Treves, Cologne, Utrecht, Fulda, and many others. In all he established fifty schools and fostered general education. After his death the schools again fell into the control of the clergy, and education for the masses was neglected.

IX. CHRISTIAN LIFE AND WORSHIP.

This is the period of the Dark Ages, and the Christian life is at a low ebb, in spite of the few great men—including Gregory and Charlemagne—which the age produced.

FROM GREGORY TO CHARLEMAGNE

1. Church Festivals. The heathen had many festivals in honor of their gods, so now these same festivals are held but under Christian names—festivals of the Assumption, Nativity, Circumcision of Jesus, Ascension, All Saints, etc.

2. There Was a Great Increase in superstition, legalism and general immorality in the Church. The priests were ignorant and corrupt. Many were guilty of heinous crimes.

3. Ecclesiasticism. Religion became more and more an outward form—kneeling before an altar, saying (not praying) prayers; pilgrimages, penances, masses for the dead, ordeals and confessions.

4. Monasticism. The monasteries contained about the only true piety of the age. The Benedictine system became the model of the West. The monks fostered missionary activity, learning, agriculture and good morals. Later they became wealthy and corrupt.

QUESTIONS.

1. When was the fall of Rome? What did Charlemagne do?

2. What was the effect of the gift of land to the pope? What great question was raised by this act?

QUESTIONS

3. What constitutes the greatness of Pope Gregory the Great?

4. Name the important missionary endeavors of this period.

5. Describe the rise of Mohammedanism. What does it stand for? What effect did it have on the Church?

6. Who was the first bishop of Rome to claim the rights of pope? What led to this claim?

7. Describe the doctrinal controversies of this period.

8. Tell about the culture and founding of schools.

9. What was the nature of the life of the Dark Ages? The worship?

CHAPTER V.

From Charlemagne to Gregory VII. 814 to 1073 A. D.

I. POLITICS.

Charlemagne died January 28, 814, and was buried in the cathedral which he built in Aachen (Aix-la-Chapelle). He was succeeded by his son Ludwig, who was a pious mollycoddle. The empire was divided in 843 by the Treaty of Verdun among Ludwig's three sons. All the successors in the Carolingian line were weak, so the splendid movements inaugurated by Charlemagne soon died out. Because of the weakness of these emperors the popes more and more encroached upon the civil rights.

On February 2, 962, Otto I. was crowned emperor by the pope. Otto was a German. He was a strong emperor and again put the empire of the West upon its feet. This is the beginning of the "Holy Roman Empire."

Feudalism arises in this period and reaches its height in the thirteenth century.

The empire became practically pulverized

into small fiefs, with their lords and vassals. This was a political and social institution which fostered individualism, broke down the papal monarchy and saved the State. In due time feudalism had served its purpose, and gave way to the new nationalism of the fourteenth century.

II. CHURCH AND STATE.

During the days of Charlemagne the emperor was supreme over Church and State. But his weak successors yielded in almost every point to papal aggression, until the end of this period we have the theory of papal supremacy in all things. The pope held that, as the successor of Peter, he wielded the two swords of Peter; viz., the Church and State. Hence the emperor is but a servant of the pope, who owns the earth.

The emperor, however, still invested the offices, both temporal and spiritual. Since the bishops and prelates got their offices from the emperor, naturally they were more of politicians than prophets. Simony was universal, and corruption, like a festering gangrene, brought the church up to her lowest ebb, in this period.

Private wars, fights, duels and interminable strife existed everywhere. The Church in Southern France tried to stop this condition. The clergy attempted to enforce (1026) the "Peace of God," forbidding all Christians to fight on penalty of excommunication. This was too stringent for the times, so they compromised (1031) with the "Truce of God," which forbade all fightings on Church festivals and from Wednesday evening till Monday morning of each week. This had a great effect in bettering conditions.

III. MISSIONS.

1. Denmark. In 822 Ebbo, Archbishop of Rheims, went to Denmark and established a successful mission there. In 826 Harold of Jutland and his retinue were baptized. Ansgar, the "Apostle of the North" (801-865), is the one through whom the conversion of the Scandinavians is largely due. He began in 826, went to Sweden (831) and became Archbishop of Hamburg (833). Persecutions, wars, and pirates opposed the missionary work and almost demolished it, but by the time of Ansgar's death (865) the missions were in a flourishing condition. "In 1075 the public services of Thor and

Odin were all absolutely interdicted by a royal order, and the cause of Christianity henceforth was everywhere triumphant." (Hardwick, p. 108.)

2. Iceland. Iceland was colonized by Norwegians in 870. In 981 a mission was started, but failed. In 996 Stefner, a native of Iceland, who became a Christian in Norway, carried back the Gospel to his people. In the year 1000 Christianity was legally established, all were immersed in the warm waters of the geysers, and paganism was abolished.

3. Greenland. Lief, of Iceland, carried the Gospel to Greenland in 999, "and in 1055 the community of Christians had been fully organized by the appointment of a bishop."

4. The Slavic Races. The Gospel was taken to the Moravians (862) by Cyril and Methodius of the Greek Church. They labored under great difficulties and opposition. Later the Moravian missions are under the bishops of Bohemia. From 871, on, the Bohemians come under the influence of the Gospel, and a century later they seem to be wholly evangelized. The Poles and the Wends come under the missionary influence from about 950 on.

5. Hungary was evangelized from 970 to 1038.

IV. OPPOSITION AND PERSECUTION OF THE CHURCH.

1. Danish and Norwegian Vikings (pirates) settled in England and harassed the people and the Church (787) for three centuries. In about 870 they settled in France, and laid waste the country. They gradually yielded to the Gospel.

2. Mohammedans. From 850 to 960 the Moslems persecuted the Christians in Spain, where multitudes perished by the scourge or in the flames like the ancient martyrs.

V. CHURCH DOCTRINE.

1. In 831 Paschasius Radbertus wrote a book, " De Corpore et Sanguine Domini," in which he declared that the bread and wine of the eucharist are changed into the real flesh and blood of Christ when consecrated by the priest, i. e., transubstantiation. In 844, when a second edition appeared, Ratramus, a monk of Corbey, criticised the view, holding that Christ is present only spiritually. Radbertus had written only what nearly everybody already believed, so the transubstantiation theory won the victory and is held today by the Catholic Church.

2. Free Will. Gottschalk (c. 847) held that man is predestined in everything; some to heaven, others to hell. Man is predestined to grace, or to sin; he has no free will at all. This aroused his former teacher at Fuldo, Rabanus Maurus, who believed in Divine decrees, but could not bear making God responsible for sin. Gottschalk was put into prison, remaining till his death (868).

3. John Scatus Erigena. Erigena was one of the precursors of the schoolmen, who tried to establish Christian dogmas by philosophy. He believed (as all the schoolmen) that philosophy and theology are the same, and human reason could and should substantiate religion. This learned philosopher was asked to write on the two mooted questions of the day, Predestination and the Eucharist. His former treatise appeared in 851, wherein he defends the freedom of the will. Erigena saw no more in the Eucharist than a memorial of Christian truths, " By which the spirit of the faithful is revived, instructed and sustained." It is needless to say that by these liberal views Erigena got enemies on all sides.

4. Image Worship. This controversy arose again and waged from 815 to 879. The images gained the victory and remained in the churches as objects of adoration and worship. This controversy was opened again in the sixteenth century.

VI. THE CORRUPTION OF THE CHURCH.

1. The Papacy (from 880-1049). " The papacy lost almost all its power and prestige and came to be a bone of contention among rival factions. Pope Formosus (891-898), having been treated with the utmost indignity by one party, and having been enabled afterwards to wreak bloody vengeance upon his enemies, was probably poisoned. He was succeeded (after fifteen days, during which Boniface VI. began and ended his pontifical reign) by his mortal enemy, Stephen VI., who had his body exhumed, tried, condemned, deposed, stripped of pontifical robes, cut to pieces and thrown into the Tiber. The pontifical acts of Formosus were, of course, abrogated by Stephen. In about a year the other party triumphed, and Stephen was imprisoned and strangled. Stephen's successor, Marinus, reigned four months, and Marinus' successor three weeks. John X. was elected by the party that had sustained Formosus (898), and devoted his energies to annulling the proceedings of Stephen. Leo V. (903), having reigned for two months, was murdered by his chaplain, who succeeded him. The murderer was murdered and succeeded by Sergius III., after eight months of pontifical glory." (Newman, vol. I, p. 497.)

"With Sergius was inaugurated what is known in history as the Pornocracy. Marozia, a licentious noblewoman, as mistress of Sergius, directed the papal government for seven years. His successor, John X., was appointed by his mistress, Theodora. He led in person a successful military expedition against the Saracens, but returned to be driven into exile by Marozia. Through the influence of another licentious woman he succeeded in reinstating himself, but through the influence of Marozia he was soon afterwards strangled in a dungeon. The next three popes were creatures of

Marozia; the third (John XI.), her bastard son by Pope Sergius, a youth of twenty-one. From 936 to 956 a sort of Roman republic, with Alberic at its head, prevailed.

Alberic appointed four popes in succession and restrained them from political interference. A son of Alberic (a boy of twelve, or, as others say, eighteen), profligate beyond his years, succeeded his father in the civil government, and moreover assumed the papal office (John XII). He was charged by his contemporaries with the violation of almost every principle of morality and religion: sacrilege, adultery, violation of widows, living with his father's mistress, invocation of Jupiter and Venus, and turning the papal palace into a brothel. He was driven from the city, at the request of the people, by the aid of the German Emperor Otto, before whom he had been tried. After a time he was restored through the intervention of harlots, but was soon afterwards killed by the injured husband of a paramour." (Newman, ibid.)

2. Bishops and Priests. Like the popes, so the bishops, priests and laity were steeped in vices and sins. These ecclesiastics got their appointments from the State, and hence were mostly corrupt and ignorant politicians who had no qualifications whatever for their offices. Simony and impurity were almost universal.

VII. CENTRALIZATION.

In the last chapter we noticed the growth of papal authority. In this period one character stands out supremely as the creator of papal power and authority. Nicholas I. (858-867), like Gregory I., came to the papal throne in a time of wild disorder and general disintegration. Nicholas, also, was a man of clean morals, and a gentle disposition to those who did what was right. But he excelled all his predecessors in the conception he had of papal authority and in the use of such authority.

The false decretals (Isidorian decretals) came to hand about this time. These decretals were doubtless the fabrication of a few bishops in connivance with the pope, who chafed under the vigilant and autocratic rule of the metropolitans, or archbishops. The bishops would rather be under the pope at a distance than under the archbishops near at hand. Hence, to increase the popes' authority, they invented a num-

ber of decrees going back to 68 A. D., show-
ing that the popes (bishops of Rome) in
these early years had exercised absolute
sovereignty over all—both Church and
State. The false decrees were mixed with
authentic decrees and sent out over the
name of the great scholar, Isidore of Seville,
who died a few centuries before they appeared.

Nicholas I. used these decretals as genu-
ine (for no one doubted them till the Reformation) in a most effective manner. (1)
He humbled Hincmar, Archbishop of
Rheims, by restoring Bishop Rothbald of
Soissons, whom Hincmar had deposed.
Hincmar was compelled to apologize and
to recognize the pope's authority. (2) Lo-
thaire II., King of France, divorced his wife
and married his maid, Waldroda. The
queen, Tutberga, appealed to the pope, who
espoused the cause and brought the king
to terms. (3) He also restored Ignatius,
Patriarch of Constantinople, who had been
unjustly deposed by the Eastern emperor.

VIII. REFORM—CLUNY.

Monasticism has four great periods in
the West: (1) The Benedictines of the sixth

century, (2) the Cluny movement of the tenth century, (3) the mendicants of the thirteenth century, and (4) the Jesuits of the sixteenth century. (Harnack.) Each of these movements was a reformation at the beginning, but, having served its purpose, became corrupt. In the tenth century the monasteries lost their savor and were swept down in the general maelstrom of corruption. But just when the church most needed help a new kind of monastery came into being. In 910 Cluny, in France, was founded by Berno. Berno's successor, Odo (927-941), developed this monastery to its tremendous influence. By the middle of the twelfth century over 2,000 convents were under the control of Cluny. Hildebrand (Gregory VII.) was a monk of Cluny and carried out the Cluny reforms—celibacy of the clergy, and to put an end to simony by ending lay investiture.

IX. CHRISTIAN LIFE AND WORSHIP.

The morals of the Church have already been described. The worship had now become thoroughly developed into the Roman religion—legalism and heathenism.

Sacerdotalism, magic, formalism, ecclesiasticism, characterize the religion of the Middle Ages. Anselm, the great schoolman of the period, was canonized, so the magic and superstition of these "Dark Ages" will continue to be the religious expression of Roman Catholicism, unless the "infallible pope" can change what has already been "infallibly" declared to be infallible. Indulgences, penance, worship of relics, the bones of the saints, pilgrimages, etc., take the place of repentance and a pure heart. The laity are not taught the Scriptures, and the clergy do not know them. Ignorance, superstition and corruption prevail everywhere. But always a few men, here and there, in each generation, have been preserved, who drink from the pure source of Light and Life, who are the leaven of the kingdom which becomes the center of reform. Monasticism always stands for "renunciation of the world." The new monastic movement spells reform.

QUESTIONS.

1. Describe the political conditions of this period.

2. What was the relation of the Church and the State?

3. Describe the missionary activities to Denmark; to Iceland; to Greenland; to the Slavs.

4. Name the two sources of persecution of the Church in this period.

5. What is transubstantiation? What was the Free Will Controversy? Who was Erigena? What was the result of the image worship controversy?

6. Describe the corruption of the papacy; of the bishops and the priests.

7. What caused the growth of the centralization of the power in the pope? How did Pope Nicholas show his power?

8. What was the Cluny Reform Movement?

9. Describe the Christian life and worship.

CHAPTER VI.

From Gregory VII. to Boniface VIII. 1073 to 1294 A. D.

I. INTRODUCTION.

In 1054 the Eastern Church was definitely separated from the West. The Cluny Reform Movement became active under a number of German popes, beginning with Leo IX. (1049). Hildebrand, a young monk of Cluny, who had gone into exile with Gregory VI., was the chief adviser, and the real power that directed the popes until he himself became Pope Gregory VII., in 1073. The Cluny reformers believed that the corruption of the clergy—simony, ignorance, and impurity—could be cured by two reforms; viz., celibacy of the clergy and ecclesiastical instead of lay investiture; for many of the clergy were married, and most of them were incompetent politicians, who bought their offices from the civil rulers. Lay investiture means to be invested with the office by the civil ruler.

II. HILDEBRAND.

" During the funeral services of Alexander II. at St. John's, in the Lateran, a great shout arose from the multitude in the church that Hildebrand should be their bishop. The cardinal, Hugh the White, addressed the assembly, 'You know, brethren,' he said, 'how, since the time of Leo IX., Hildebrand has exalted the Roman Church, and freed our city. We cannot find a better pope than he. Indeed, we cannot find his equal. Let us then elect him, who, having been ordained in our Church, is known to us all, and thoroughly approved by us all.' There was a great shout in answer: 'St. Peter has chosen Hildebrand to be pope.' Despite his resistance, Hildebrand was dragged to the church of St. Peter ad Vinculo and immediately enthroned." (Tout, " The Empire and Papacy," p. 124.)

Hildebrand was a man of indomitable will, high moral sense, and a purpose to reform the world by creating " a sort of universal monarchy of the papacy." He believed that " the pope is the master of emperors; he is rendered holy by the merits of his predecessor, St. Peter; the Roman

Church has never erred, and Holy Scriptures prove that it never can err; to resist it is to resist God." Hildebrand was bent on reform, but he was too severe and legalistic in his methods. Reform cannot be effective or permanent which is merely external; legalistic morality cannot do the work of a new affection in the heart.

III. THE SYNOD OF 1075.

Gregory VII. (Hildebrand) held a synod in Rome that decided against lay investiture and simony. "If any one henceforth receive from the hand of any lay person a bishopric or abbey, let him not be considered as abbot or bishop, and let the favor of St. Peter and the gate of the Church be forbidden to him. If an emperor, a king, a duke, a count, or any other lay person presume to give investiture of any ecclesiastical dignity, let him be excommunicated." This decree was the beginning of a great contest between the emperor and the pope that lasted for several centuries.

IV. HENRY IV.

The emperor was incensed at this new decree and ignored it by investing a new bishop at Milan. In 1076 Henry IV. held a

council at Worms and condemned the pope.
Henry wrote a letter to the pope, which began as follows: " Henry, king, not by usur-
pation, but by the holy ordination of God,
to Hildebrand, not pope, but false monk."
Henry accused the pope of all kinds of sins,
and especially that he dishonored the emperor, who is divinely appointed. The letter closed thus: " I, Henry, king by the
grace of God, with all my bishops, say unto
you: Come down, come down, and be ac-
cursed through all the ages." (Thatcher
and McNeal, " Source Book.") Hereupon
the pope excommunicated the emperor and
absolved all his subjects from allegiance to
him. The pope addressed his letter to St.
Peter: " Confident of my integrity and
authority, I now declare in the name of Om-
nipotent God, the Father, Son, and Holy
Spirit, that Henry, son of the Emperor
Henry, is deprived of his kingdom of Germany and Italy; I do this by thy authority
and in defense of the honor of thy Church;
because he has rebelled against it. . . .
therefore by thy authority I place him under the curse. It is in thy name that I
curse him, that all people may know that
thou art Peter, and upon thy rock the Son
of the living God has built his church, and

the gates of hell shall not prevail against it." (Thatcher and McNeal, "Source Book.")

V. CANOSSA.

The pope's bull of excommunication had the desired effect. Henry had enemies at home and his subjects and army left him. Now Henry always seemed to know how to get out of a difficulty. He must make peace with the pope. Not waiting till the pope could come to Germany, as he had planned, and convene Henry's enemies, the emperor set out in haste to meet the pope and confess. The pope, hearing that Henry was coming, but not knowing his intent, intrenched himself in Matilda's fortress at Canossa. Gregory writes that Henry "presented himself at the gate of the castle, barefoot and clad only in wretched woollen garments, beseeching us with tears to grant him absolution and forgiveness. This he continued to do for three days, until all those about us were moved to compassion at his plight and interceded for him with tears and prayers." The pope was finally prevailed upon by Matilda to forgive Henry. Thus the emperor bowed to the pope, but it was a good stroke of policy for Henry.

VI. HENRY AND GREGORY.

Henry's success at Canossa gained for him the loyalty of Germany. But before Henry got back to Germany, the papal legates elected another king, Rudolph of Schwabia, in place of Henry. War ensued, which lasted for a few years, but left Henry victorious. Now Henry and his friends elected another pope. Henry invaded Italy (1081-84), and finally captured Rome and besieged Gregory in the castle of St. Angelo. Gregory invited the Normans of South Italy to come to Rome. Henry fled beyond the Alps, and after a four days' siege the Normans gained the city and sacked it. "Rome was ruthlessly sacked, whole quarters were burned down, hideous massacres and outrages were perpetrated, and thousands of Romans were sold as slaves." The successor of St. Peter invited this outrage, and watched from the castle of St. Angelo, without the shedding of a single tear, the dragging of helpless women from their homes who were ruthlessly outraged, then massacred. The pope finally fled to Salerno, where he died May 25, 1085.

VII. THE CRUSADES.

Jerusalem fell into the hands of the Moslem. Peter the Hermit made a pilgrimage to Jerusalem and brought back heartrending stories about the desecration of the Holy City. Pope Urban II. referred the matter of a crusade to a council, and a voice from the multitude cried out, "Deus vult" ("God wills it"). This became the watchword which electrified Europe, and everybody wanted to fight the Moslem. The pope offered total absolution to all who would make a pilgrimage in so holy a cause. Hundreds of thousands of people rushed to Palestine.

1. **The First Crusade (1095)** was headed by Peter the Hermit and Walter the Penniless with 200,000 followers. All were lost. Finally 80,000 men, under Godfrey of Bouillon, captured Antioch, Edessa, and Jerusalem (1099). Godfrey became "Protector of the Holy Sepulchre." One of the results of this crusade was the formation of new orders of soldier monks—Knight Templars, Knights of St. John, and the Teutonic Knights.

2. **The Second Crusade (1147)** was a stupendous failure. It was led by Louis VII.

of France, and Conrad III. of Germany.
Bernard of Clairvaux urged this crusade,
and comforted himself for the loss of three
great armies by saying that it was better
for them to die in a good cause and go to
heaven, than to remain at home in sin and
be lost eternally.

3. The Third Crusade (1187) was the
most splendid flower of feudalism and chivalry. It was led by the greatest knights of
Europe, in their most gorgeous attire and
display. Richard, Cœur de Lion, King of
England; Philip Augustus, King of France;
and Frederick Barbarossa, the Roman Emperor, were the leaders. Jealousies between
the leaders were fatal to success. They accomplished nothing except to free the Christians who lived in Jerusalem from paying
taxes.

4. In 1204 a Crusade was led by Venice
against Constantinople, purely for selfish
reasons. In 1212 the fanaticism of Europe
led to a " Children's Crusade," which resulted in the death and slavery of about 50,-
000 children. All the later crusades were
failures, so far as the original purpose was
concerned—to rescue the Holy City from
the Moslem.

VIII. RESULTS OF THE CRUSADES.

1. "The breaking up of feudalism and the development of nationality."

2. "Increase of wealth and power of the papacy."

3. "The opening up of commerce."

4. "The general diffusion of enlightenment."

5. "The building up of great commercial cities whose interest lay in opposing feudalism and in promoting freedom of thought."

6. "The crusades tended to fuse Christendom into a homogeneous mass by uniting it into a common cause." (Newman, vol. I, p. 462.)

IX. INNOCENT III. (1198-1216), PAPAL SUPREMACY.

In Innocent III. we find the papacy at its height in absolutism. Innocent was one of the ablest of the popes, and had back of him the added strength of Hildebrand and the crusades, which made the pope dictator of kings and emperors. His theory of the papacy was expressed in these words: "The vicegerent of Christ is less than God and more than man. God has given to St. Peter not only the government of the church, but also the government of the world. The Church is the sun, the empire the moon, shining with borrowed light."

1. Innocent Put France under the interdict because Philip Augustus put away his wife. Philip came to terms.

2. He Excommunicated Otto IV. of Germany and absolved his subjects (1211), because he showed a spirit of independence. Otto retired to private life.

3. Innocent Brought King John of England to his knees, took away his kingdom (1213), then gave it back as a fief. The people of England forced the Magna Charta from King John (1215), and the pope fortunately died before he could reverse it.

X. NEW SECTS.

1. The Albigenses lived in southern France. They rejected much of the Roman doctrine, especially the formalism. Their aim was to purify religion and make it more spiritual. But they went too far and became involved in gnostic and Manichæan dualism. They were completely exterminated by a crusade sent against them by the pope, who offered absolution to all who took part in the crusade.

2. The Waldenses. About 1170 Peter Waldo of Lyons, France, and his followers began to preach the Gospel to the people. They procured a translation of the Gospel in the vernacular. They rejected Catholic formalism, prayers for the dead, and the mass, and attempted to get back to apostolic Christianity. They emphasized holy living and not formalism as the essence of religion. The Waldenses were excommunicated in 1184, and became, throughout their history, the object of the most cruel persecutions known to mankind.

XI. MENDICANTS.

Many new orders came into being, to offset the corruption of the older orders and of the Church. The Cistercians (1098) became famous through Bernard of Clairvaux. The Carthusians were noted for their rigid discipline. The Order of St. Anthony was principally engaged in the care of the sick. But the two orders of the most prominence are the Mendicants.

The Dominicans, or Black Friars, were founded by St. Dominic (1170-1221), who tried to convert the Albigenses in southern France. The Dominicans became the agents of the pope during the Inquisition.

The Franciscans, or Grey Friars, were founded by St. Francis of Assisi (1182-1226). The life of St. Francis is one of the most interesting in all church history. He had been a reckless, worldly youth and a spendthrift. A severe illness made him thoughtful and caused his conversion. He became prodigal in almsgiving, and he chose poverty for his bride. He went about almost naked, barefooted, and hungry, preaching the Gospel to the people. His great passion was love and sympathy. Possibly no one since Christ has impressed the people with such an overflowing love as did Francis of Assisi.

The fundamental difference between the earlier orders and the Mendicants was that the former tried to save the individual soul by running away from the world, while the latter tried to save the world by mingling with the world.

XII. SCHOLASTICISM.

Scholasticism, as well as papal supremacy, comes to its culmination in this period, and reaches its climax in the thirteenth century. " Scholasticism is but another name for the mediæval system of dogmatics." It is philosophy and logic applied to the subject matter of theology; attempting to define and base the dogmas of the Church in **reason**. Scholasticism was actuated by a zeal for the Catholic Church, which it tried to defend by an elaborate system of philosophy. The principles of Aristotle were largely made the basis of scholasticism.

The most important men of this period were Anselm (d. 1109), Abelard (d. 1142), Peter Lombard (d. 1164), Alexander Hales (d. 1245), Albertus Magnus (d. 1280), Thomas Aquinas (d. 1274), Bonaventura (d. 1274), and Duns Scotus (d. 1308). Only a few of these can be considered here.

1. Anselm, Archbishop of Canterbury, made a great contribution to the doctrine of the atonement in his book, " Cur Deus Homo " (" Why the God-Man "). For a thousand years the Church held that Christ's death was a ransom paid to Satan to buy back humanity which Satan had gotten by the fall of man. The doctrine of Anselm may be summed up as follows: (1) God's relation to man is that of a feudal lord or suzerain; he must be honored. (2) Sin is robbing God of the honor due him, and all sin must be punished or satisfied. (3) Sin is measured not by the act, but by the greatness or dignity of him against whom the sin is committed; hence the least dishonor against an infinite God demands an infinite punishment or death. (4) God's justice demands such punishment; his mercy leans toward forgiveness; the parallelogram of forces results in vicarious sacrifice. (5) God's love prepared the God-Man, Christ, who was perfectly obedient and needed no punishment for himself; hence his death is an infinite reward which is substituted for man's just punishment, whereby man is released. (6) Thus God's honor is satisfied by Christ's substitutionary suffering, and man is saved.

2. Abelard rested the atonement entirely upon the love and benevolence of God. God's love and forgiveness lose all meaning if he exacts payment.

3. Peter Lombard wrote four books of sentences, " To put forth the strength of the church's faith; to make plain the meaning of the holy sacraments."

4. Thomas Aquinas (1227-74) was probably the greatest of the scholastics. His " Summa Totius Theologiæ " (" The Sum of All Theology ") has been canonized as the theology of the Catholic Church, and is the basis of that church at the present time. Thus the Roman Church rests upon mediæval theology.

5. John Duns Scotus was a great rival of Aquinas in intellectual power. He differed widely from Aquinas in theology and became the forerunner of later Nominalism.

XIII. MYSTICISM.

Bernard of Clairvaux (1091-1153) became a monk at the Cistercian Monastery at Citeaux. He was a young man of all the charms, ability and prestige needed to give him the highest positions in State and society. He entered the most exacting monastery in the world, and went even beyond the requirements of the monastery in self-discipline. Bernard succeeded in getting all his warrior brethren into the monastery except the youngest, who was not old enough to enter. Bernard was one of the greatest orators and most persuasive preachers in the history of the Church. Society was rough, lawless, corrupt; from this Bernard was calling men, both by the eloquence of his voice and by the still greater eloquence of his pure and holy life.

In 1115 Bernard, with twelve others, was sent forth from Citeaux to found another monastery, which he established at Clairvaux. This place had been a marshy valley called "Valley of Wormwood." Now it was called Clairvaux, or Bright Valley.

Bernard later entered into public life, preaching against luxury and worldliness. He boldly attacked all sin, whether in the papacy, the bishops, priests or laymen. He opposed Abelard by putting his own mystical faith in the certainties of religion over against the speculations of the schoolmen. This was a struggle between giants—constructive, practical faith against critical, speculative reason. St. Bernard was victorious in this contest. Bernard is classed among the mystics because of his contemplative nature, believing that divine truth comes to one by resignation and contemplation; the mystic, intuitive vision rather than by speculative reason.

XIV. CHRISTIAN LIFE AND WORSHIP.

The general corruption of the ministry of the Church has already been referred to—simony and concubinage. Lay investiture was finally settled by a compromise at the Concordat of Worms in 1122, when Henry V. gave up the right of investiture.

Papal supremacy, which was begun by Gregory VII. (1073), reached its climax in Innocent III. (1198-1216), and continued to Boniface VIII. (1294). The morals of the people were low; life was wild, lawless and corrupt.

The Church became more and more ceremonial. Seven sacraments now composed the system; viz., baptism, confirmation, eucharist, penance, extreme unction, marriage, and ordination. There was also an increase in the worship of saints and relics; of pilgrimages, absolution, indulgences, etc. The belief in a " treasury of merit " developed. This meant that the saints had more merit than was necessary for their salvation, and the balance of their merit could be transferred by the pope to those who needed it upon the payment of a certain sum of money. Religion became more and more external.

Fortunately, during all the periods of the Dark Ages there were always some noble men and women who were real saints that became the good seed for the revival of a new conscience, and the hope of a truer religion. The Schoolmen, the Mystics, the Monks, all having shortcomings of their own, nevertheless each contributed toward a new point of view that was destined to free human thought, and enthrone spiritual religion for the people.

QUESTIONS.

1. What reforms were necessary in the Church?

2. Who was Hildebrand? Describe his character.

3. What was done at the Synod of 1075?

4. Who was the Roman Emperor?

5. What took place at Canossa? What is the significance of this event?

6. Describe the conflict between Henry and Gregory.

7. What were the Crusades? Describe the first three.

8. Name four results of the Crusades.

9. What is meant by papal supremacy? What did the pope do that shows his supremacy over the temporal powers?

10. Who were the Albigenses? The Waldenses?

11. Name the two Mendicant orders of supreme importance. How did the Mendicants differ from the earlier orders?

12. What was Scholasticism? Name the great schoolmen.

QUESTIONS

13. What is Mysticism? Tell some facts about Bernard of Clairvaux.

14. What were the morals of the Church during this period? What can you say about the worship?

CHAPTER VII.

From Boniface VIII. to Luther's Theses, 1294 to 1517 A. D.

I. CHURCH AND STATE.

Pope Boniface VIII. (1294-1303) tried to rule with the same autocratic power as did Innocent III. But the times changed. After the crusades a spirit of nationality developed, and strong civil rulers, especially of England and France, resisted the monarchial claims of the papacy. During the crusades the pope was the inevitable head of Europe; but public sentiment now began to turn its attention to political and national independence and glory. In this period the papacy fell, never again to regain its supremacy as in the thirteenth century.

Feudalism and chivalry, too, came to an end by the new spirit of nationalism, the formation of standard armies, the introduction of gunpowder, and the new interest in commerce.

This was a period of great unrest and

change politically; wars ravaged all Europe. The Hundred Years' War tried to settle the question whether England was to rule Scotland and France. Constantinople fell into the hands of the Moslem in 1453. The Moors in Spain fell in 1492. The same year Columbus discovered America.

II. THE BABYLONIAN CAPTIVITY
(1305-1376).

Pope Boniface VIII. was made arbitrator of a dispute between Philip the Fair of France and Edward of England. Philip did not like the pope's decision. The pope claimed to have complete authority over the State as well as over the Church.

Philip seized the pope and put him in prison, where he died. The next pope, Benedict XI. (1303-1304), reigned only nine months, when he died. He was succeeded by Clement V., a Frenchman, who was subject to the king, and made his papal residence in Avignon, France, instead of at Rome, as did all his predecessors. The papacy remained at Avignon for seventy years (1305-1376).

This period is called the Babylonian Captivity, in correspondence to the seventy years that the Jews were in Babylon.

These popes at Avignon were all under French influence, lived like rich lords, in a most worldly fashion, spent their time in political intrigues, and, in general, lacked spirituality. They invented new ways by which they might enrich themselves. This new worldliness of the popes, and their subserviency to French interests, lost for the papacy the respect of the people. There was general decline of the papacy, while the empire gained power.

III. THE GREAT SCHISM.

Pope Gregory XI. (1370-1378) was influenced by Catherine of Siena to return to Rome and thus end the Captivity (1376). Urban VI. was elected at his death (1378), with the understanding that he return to Avignon. This he refused to do, so the French cardinals, who had the majority, elected Clement VII. at Avignon. Urban's proud, overbearing and cruel spirit alienated the cardinals from him, and they now favored Clement. Urban appointed new cardinals, and now there were two popes with two colleges of Cardinals—one at

Rome and the other at Avignon. This schism lasted forty years (1378-1417).

This schism brought the Church into bad repute, so that all the better people began to use their influence to end this shame and disgrace of the Church. The University of Paris took the lead in healing the schism. Several propositions were made. (1) That one or both of the popes should resign and make way for a new pope. (2) That a general council should be called to end the schism. Since neither of the popes yielded his claims, a council was called at Pisa in 1409.

IV. THE COUNCIL OF PISA.

The College of Cardinals called this council, and in this very act struck a blow at the doctrine of papal autocracy. The two popes were deposed and Alexander V. was elected pope, with the promise that he would work reforms. The two popes refused to withdraw, hence the result was three popes. Alexander V. died in 1410 and was succeeded by John XXIII., a mercenary politician. Things were going from bad to worse, and John had to yield to the Emperor Sigismund to call a new council.

V. THE COUNCIL OF CONSTANCE
(1414-18).

This was the sixteenth Œcumenical Council of the Church and the largest in attendance. It brought together 18,000 priests and 100,000 strangers. Sigismund, the emperor, was, in reality, the mover and leader of the council. He was anxious to end the schism. John XXIII. was tried for his many crimes, and deposed. Seventy charges of criminality were brought against him. Gregory XII. (of Rome) and Benedict XIII. (of Avignon) also were deposed. Martin V. was elected pope (1417), and thus ended the schism. But Martin did not carry out the reforms which he promised.

The Council of Constance made itself infamous by the condemnation and burning at the stake of John Huss, and his friend, Jerome of Prague (July 6, 1415). This council also condemned the writings of Wiclif, and ordered his bones to be burned and the ashes scattered upon the waters.

VI. THE COUNCIL OF BASLE (1431-49).

Martin V. (1417-31) was a strong pope, but the corruptions were too deep-seated to reform them all at once; neither was the pope strongly inclined to do so. Pope Eugenius IV. (1431-47) organized this council, which attempted (1) to exterminate the heretics, and (2) to purify the Church. It also attempted to unite the Eastern and Western Churches. The council accomplished nothing worth while. It was too weak to adjourn and finally died of inanity.

VII. THE WICKED POPES.

Paul II. (1464-71) was opposed to the progress and learning instituted by Nicholas V. He was proud and avaricious. Sixtus IV. (1471-84) was more of a territorial lord or duke than head of the Church. " Sixtus is reported to have had sixteen illegitimate children, whose interest he advanced, using his office to this end." (Zenos, " Compendium of Church History," p. 186.)

" **Innocent VIII.** (1484-92) abased the papacy no less than his predecessors. His care was to promote and to enrich his numerous children. To this end offices were sold with perfect shamelessness." (Sheldon, " The Mediæval Church.")

Alexander VI. (1492-1503) represents the climax of papal degradation. He bought his office, and robbed everybody he could to advance his illegitimate children. "Alexander sold the keys, the altars, and Christ." He was doubtless guilty of poisoning others to get their wealth, and finally drank the poison prepared by his son.

The immorality of these popes, and their increased clamor for money, which they got through the sale of indulgences, did much to arouse the people, which resulted in the Reformation.

VIII. HUMANISM.

This period might be called "Humanism," as the next is called "Reformation." Humanism means a just appreciation of man. The fourth and fifth centuries were concerned with the problems of Christology, the fourteenth and fifteenth with anthropology, and the sixteenth, with soteriology. This period is also called the Renaissance. It is a new birth in literature, art, and philosophy, especially a revival in the Greek classics.

Dante, Petrarch, and Boccaccio represented the new birth in literature; Ciambue and Giotto in art; Pletho and Ficino advanced Greek studies and philosophy.

The influence of the Renaissance is one of the prime causes of the Reformation.

IX. MYSTICISM.

In the twelfth century, Bernard of Clairvaux and William of Champeaux were representative mystics. In this period a number of causes led to the contemplative life which sought and found peace and victory in mysticism.

The Neo-Platonism, still in the Church, the aridity of Scholasticism, the corruption of the hierarchy, the ravages of the black death, and the natural convulsions of earthquakes—all drove men to quiet contemplation.

The great mystics were: Meister Eckart (1260-1327), John Tauler (1290-1361), Ruysbroek (1298-1386), and Thomas à Kempis (1380-1471). All these mystics remained faithful to the Catholic Church. "The Friends of God" were a small sect of mystics who drifted from the organized Church.

X. LIFE AND WORSHIP.

Boniface VIII. proclaimed the year 1300 to be a jubilee year. All who made pilgrimages to Rome received absolution. Two hundred thousand people came to Rome and contributed freely to the pope's income. This proved to be profitable for the popes, so jubilees became more frequent.

Indulgences were granted at first, only for the remission of a part of one's sins upon the payment of a certain sum of money to the Church. Afterwards the whole penalty for sin could be paid with money; and finally the sins of the future could be paid for in anticipation.

The corruption of the Church was general, religion was formal and external, symbolism and magic took the place of morality and spirituality. Only in the case of mystics, the reforming sects, and the great prophets of the new age, do we find a light to the world and the salt of the earth.

The Inquisition, in the hands of the Dominicans, was developed to its highest perfection in Spain. It was a secret order, which sought out heretics, tortured and killed them, and confiscated their property. Persons accused were given, as a rule, no trial, and thousands of innocent Christians and Jews suffered the most horrible tortures and death.

XI. THE FORERUNNERS OF THE REFORMATION.

I. Wiclif (1320-1384). Wiclif was born in England, educated at Merton College, Oxford, and became Fellow and Warden of Balliol (1361). In 1374 he went to Lutterworth, where the greatest scholar in England became an itinerant missionary preacher. He lived the simple life and preached to the masses.

Wiclif wrote on theology, politics, and religious reform. His political writings attracted wide attention. He held to the separation of Church and State. Both rest upon the supreme sovereignty of God. Wiclif denied the authority of the pope; all authority rests in God.

England had been overrun by the beggar monks. They held that poverty was in itself merit. Wiclif opposed this idea. Poverty is not in itself merit, but a means to a deeper, richer, spiritual life. In all his religious writings he advocated reform.

In 1380 Wiclif began the translation of the Bible. This made it possible for the Scriptures to reach the people.

He differed from the Catholic Church on the eucharist, denying transubstantiation.

He held that Christ was present after the consecration of the elements, but they remained bread and wine as before.

Wiclif was the founder of English prose. He was accused of heresy, tried without much success and persecuted. In 1384 he was asked to appear before the pope at Rome, but his poor health prevented his going. He wrote to the pope that he would gladly explain his teaching to anyone, and especially to the pope, "because," he wrote, "I suppose that if it be orthodox, he will confirm it with all humility, and if it be erroneous, he will correct it." He declared he learned from the Scriptures to follow the pope only so far as he (the pope) followed Christ.

2. John Hus (1369-1415). John Hus was a peasant boy of Bohemia, whose character was moulded by a number of influences. He inherited a deep spiritual and moral sense, studied the Scriptures carefully, read the books of Wiclif, and he added to these his love of the simple life, the preaching of the Gospel, and a burning hatred of the corruptions in the Church.

There were also other men before Hus, in Bohemia, who had caught the vision of a spiritual religion, who inspired the young prophet. Hus was a student at Prague, where he received his master's degree in 1396. He became dean of the faculty in 1401, and rector in 1403.

In 1400 he became a priest, and preached in a chapel called Bethlehem, in the Bohemian language. Hus was a pure, noble man of a winning personality.

Hus had a friend, Jerome of Prague, who was very eloquent. They put all authority in the Scriptures.

Hus wanted to reform the Church. His method was, like that of Jesus, from below, by preaching the pure Gospel. Christ is the head of the Church, and spirituality is the measure of the Christian.

Hus was forbidden to preach in Bethlehem Chapel, was asked to burn the books of Wiclif, and finally (1411) was excommunicated. In 1412 the pope put an interdict upon Prague against Hus. He left the city to save the people.

When Sigismund called the Council of Constance, Hus was ready to go and defend himself. The emperor promised safe conduct thither and return. When Hus arrived at Constance he and Jerome were cast into prison. Six months later came the trial. Hus was charged with heresy. But none of the charges could be found in any of his writings nor in his public expressions. But the council decided he was a heretic, and he must recant. Recant of what? Can a man confess to a sin which he did not commit? Sigismund advised him to admit heresy, then recant and save his life. How could he admit a thing which was not true? Hus had a conscience. "Indeed it is better for me to die, than, by avoiding a momentary punishment, to fall into the hands of the Lord, and perhaps afterwards into fire and everlasting punishment." Hus was a martyr to conscience.

On July 6, 1415, he and Jerome were burned at the stake, as martyrs to the truth. Why were they burned? Because they refused to tell a lie, even though a church council asked them to do so. Church councils sometimes err.

3. Savonarola (1452-1498). Savonarola became a Dominican monk at twenty-two at Bologna. In 1491 he became prior of St. Mark's Monastery in Florence, having been there nine years. Savonarola was a great preacher. He rebuked (1) the corruption of the laity and clergy, (2) the lack of spirituality in an age of luxury and culture, (3) the luxury of common life and the pomp of religious worship.

He was opposed to the autocratic rule of the Medici in Florence, and worked for freedom. He resolved to restore the liberties of Florence. In 1494 Savonarola became ruler of the city. He effected a great moral and religious reform in the city. As prior of the monastery, he caused a great moral reformation, and converted it into a school to study the Scriptures and art.

Savonarola opposed the pope, Alexander, who got his office by bribery. The pope tried to quiet him by offering him a cardinalate. He refused, saying that he would never wear the red hat unless it were dyed in his own blood of martyrdom.

In 1497, at the time of the carnival, he sent the boys of Florence to the homes of the people to ask for vanities or luxuries. They made a pile fifteen stories high of " carnival masks, and dresses, rich dresses and ornaments of women, false hair, dice, cards, perfumes, and cosmetics, amatory poems and other books of a free character, musical instruments, paintings, sculptures," and all other things which were associated with worldliness and immorality, and burned them. Instead of the usual frivolities of the carnival, Savonarola and his boys marched through the streets and sang songs and psalms.

On May 12, 1497, he was excommunicated. He continued preaching and denounced the pope. Jealousy arose among the Franciscans. Savonarola was challenged to an ordeal by fire, whereby he was to prove or free himself of guilt. Guilt of what? That was not asked—only guilt. A storm prevented the ordeal by fire. The people took this as an evil omen and turned against him. Savonarola was tortured and his weak frame broke down. His enemies got control of the city. On May 20, 1498, Savonarola and three of his friends were hanged, then burned. Why? Because he broke down under inhuman torture. Or better, because he followed in the footsteps of his Lord, in bearing witness to the truth.

While Savonarola was being burned, young Luther was in preparation to lead the forces of truth and freedom to victory. The Reformation is on.

BONIFACE VIII. TO LUTHER'S THESES

QUESTIONS.

1. What change takes place in the power of the papacy? What changes in civic life are being made? Describe the spirit of the age.

2. Describe the Babylonian Captivity of the Church.

3. What was the Great Schism? What was its effect on the Church?

4. What efforts were made to heal the schism? What was done at the Council of Pisa?

5. Who called the Council of Constance? How was the schism ended? What crime was committed by the Church?

6. Describe the Council of Basle.

7. Who were the "wicked popes"? Describe their character. What effect did their lives have upon later history?

8. What was Humanism?

9. What is Mysticism? Name the great Mystics.

10. Describe the Christian life and worship.

11. Who were the great forerunners of the Reformation? State a few facts about Wiclif; Hus; Savonarola.

CHAPTER VIII.

The Reformation, 1517 to 1648 A. D.

I. INTRODUCTION.

Modern history begins with the discovery of America by Columbus in 1492; modern Church history with the Reformation (1517). These epochs are not abrupt changes, but gradual developments. It was the modern spirit before these events that made them possible. The Reformation is mediæval in spirit and method, rather than modern; but the struggle for freedom received an impetus in the Reformation which has changed the course of history.

Three great inventions prepared the way for the Reformation. (1) Printing, with movable type, was invented about 1450. This made possible the spread of the new learning of the Renaissance. The Bible was printed and became more generally known. From 1456 to 1518 fourteen editions of the German Bible, four of the Dutch, and ninety-eight of the Latin, were published. (2) Gunpowder made the peasant equal to the mailed knight, broke down chivalry and feudalism, and furthered nationalism and the standing army. (3) The mariner's compass enabled seamen to traverse the oceans in search of new worlds. In Egypt and Babylon commerce was limited to the rivers; in Europe to the inland seas, especially the Mediterranean; now we have ocean commerce, touching the world.

Politically, a new nationalism had taken possession of Europe. Spain was the foremost power, which was united by Ferdinand and Isabella, whose grandson became Emperor Charles V. (1519). France was consolidated and was ruled by Francis I. England was the first of the great nations to be consolidated.

Italy and Germany were still divided into petty sovereignties. The popes of Rome, for selfish reasons, fostered the jealousies and quarrels between these princes, thus preventing their national unity.

II. CAUSES OF THE REFORMATION.

1. Intellectual. Humanism prepared the minds of men to question the old order of things through the revival of learning. The great humanists of this age are John Colet

(1466-1519), Desiderius Erasmus (1467-1536), who published a Greek Testament with the Latin in 1516 (Erasmus was the greatest of the humanists), Thomas More (1478-1535) the author of "Utopia," and John Renchlin, the greatest Hebrew scholar of the age.

Copernicus (1473-1543), who discovered the true idea about our solar system, also belongs to this period.

The revival of art was developed by Raphael, Michel Angelo and Da Vinci.

2. Religious. The mystics of the previous period showed the possibility of a deeper religious life. A new religious sense was created in the hearts of many of the best people in all nations who demanded a reform of the Church.

3. Corruption of the Church. Pope Alexander VI. was totally corrupt and worldly, and Julius II. was a warrior prince. The leaders of the Church everywhere were immoral, worldly, and selfish.

4. Ecclesiastical. Pope Leo X. found the treasury empty, and needed much money to carry out his plans, especially the building of St. Peter's at Rome. In accordance with former practices, he offered indulgences to the public for the purpose of raising money. Tetzel was one of the agents who greatly abused this practice, and aroused the hatred of Luther. The whole system of worship had became external, formal, and magical.

5. Economic and Political. Maximilian, the emperor, complained that the pope's income was a hundred times greater than his own. The whole of Europe was drained by taxes, annates and offerings, to satisfy the papal coffers. The economic and political unrest and dissatisfaction of Europe prevented the religious eruption from being crushed in embryo.

The spirit of nationalism, craving independence from the autocracy of the pope, was a prime factor in the Reformation.

6. Social. There was a social unrest among the peasants, who had been oppressed by the popes and princes. This, combined with other causes, united with any movement that meant change and was hopeful of a better future.

No doubt the main emphasis must always be placed in the moral and religious conscience that opposed a corrupted Church.

Ulrich von Hutten was the leader of the social movement.

III. LUTHER. 1483-1546

1. Up to 1517. Luther was born November 10, 1483, at Eisleben. His parents were humble peasants. They lived at Mansfeld, but went to Eisleben to attend a fair, " when their son was unexpectedly born on the eve of St. Martin." He was baptized the next morning and named Martin, in honor of the day. This period is summed up by Tulloch: " The boy at Mansfeld, the scholar at Eisenach, the student and monk at Erfurt, the pilgrim to Rome, the professor and preacher at Wittenberg." While at Eisenach he went from house to house and sang songs for bread. Frau Cotta took pity upon him and provided him a home.

He attended the university at Erfurt, where he studied philosophy and Latin. He received his master's degree in 1505, at the age of twenty-two. He studied law for a few years, but a dangerous illness and the sudden death of a friend turned him toward the monastery, which he entered July 16, 1505. This was an Augustinian monastery, noted for its discipline. Here Luther went through the most terrible struggles of his soul to get peace. Like Paul, he outdid others in the strict performance of the rules, but got no peace. Staupitz, the vicar, helped Luther to see that he was making too much out of little imaginary sins, and he must **believe** that God had forgiven him. Luther gained the victory through faith.

In 1508 Luther was called to the new university at Wittenberg as professor. Instead of lecturing on dry scholastic philosophy he taught the Psalms, and later, the Pauline Epistles, Romans and Galatians.

In 1511 Luther made a trip to Rome on business for his order. He was a zealous and devout Catholic in every respect. He fell at the feet of the pope with all the adoration of a pilgrim to a holy shrine. But, contrary to his expectations, instead of finding piety and reverence, he found luxury, selfishness, corruption. He, too, tried to ascend the twenty-eight steps of the Scala Santa on his knees to gain absolution, but the text, " The just shall live by faith," came to him with such power that he turned back.

On October 31, 1517, Luther nailed on the door of Castle Church (Schloss Kirche) ninety-five theses in opposition to the abuses in the sale of indulgences. The best minds in Germany agreed with Luther that Tetzel went too far in his traffic. The moral and religious conscience of Luther was aroused, and he aroused Europe.

2. **From 1517 to 1521.** The pope, at first, took no notice of this opposition, considering it a mere " squabble of monks," for Luther was an Augustinian, and Tetzel a Dominican. But all Germany was aroused.

In 1518 several fruitless attempts were made by the pope's agent, Cajetan, to make Luther retract. Finally Miltitz succeeded in making a truce. Luther promised to remain quiet if his enemies would do the same. But they did not and the discussion was renewed.

In 1519 Eck, on the papal side, debated with Luther at Leipzig. Eck forced Luther to confess that both popes and councils had erred. Hus was burned for holding such doctrines. Excommunication was sure.

In 1520, before the bull of excommunication was sent, Luther wrote three important documents: (1) "Address to the German Nobility," (2) " The Babylonian Captivity of the Church," (3) " Christian Freedom." In these he set forth his doctrines of justification by faith, the universal priesthood of all believers, the independence of Germany from papal rule, etc. The pope's bull was taken and publicly burned.

In 1521 the imperial diet met at Worms, to which Luther was summoned. He was promised safe conduct to Worms and back. Luther made his defense before the emperor, Charles V., refusing to retract any of his writings unless he was shown by Scripture or reason that he was in error. "I can and will retract nothing, for it is neither safe nor expedient to act against conscience. Here I stand; I can do no otherwise: God help me! Amen."

3. From 1521 Till His Death. On Luther's return from Worms he was captured by friends and taken to the strong castle, the Wartburg, at Eisenach, in seclusion. Here he translated the New Testament from the Greek. Previous German Testaments had been made from the Vulgate.

Disorders and extravagances at Wittenberg called him back in spite of the danger.

On June 16, 1525, Luther was married to Katharine von Bora, a former nun. The Catholics thought the antichrist would now be born.

142

Luther, Melanchthon and a few others translated the Old Testament, and the entire Bible was published in German in 1534. Luther made the prophets and apostles speak German, and was, through his Bible, and other writings, the creator of the German language, especially prose.

In 1529 Luther had a debate with Zwingli, the great Swiss reformer, in Marburg, on the Eucharist. Unfortunately, Luther was too narrow here, holding on to his consubstantiation, and thus divided Protestantism.

Luther died in 1546.

IV. PROGRESS OF THE REFORMATION.

Christian worship was changed from the Latin to the German language. Preaching the Word was emphasized; a larger place was given to hymns, in German. Luther wrote many hymns and also translated the best Latin hymns. He also wrote a catechism. Worship became didactic instead of liturgical.

In 1525 the second Council of Spires voted to return to the Edict of Worms, which put Luther under the ban. The minority "protested," hence the name "Protestant."

In 1530 the diet met at Augsburg. Here the Protestants presented a statement of their belief, written by Melanchthon, which is known as the "Augsburg Confession." This is the creed of the Lutheran Church. This diet passed an edict against the Protestants, demanding that all return to Rome.

This led to the Schmalkald League, 1531, whereby the Protestant princes agreed to resist the decree of Augsburg if the emperor tried to carry out his threat.

The Turks and France again annoyed the emperor, so both parties made peace at Nurenberg in 1532.

The progress of the Protestants from the Diet of Worms (1521) till the Council of Trent (1546) was due largely to the constant troubles which the emperor had without—with France and the Turks—which prevented his interfering effectively with the Lutheran movement.

In opposition to the Schmalkald League, the Catholics formed the "Holy League" (1538).

Another conference, at Ratisbon (1541), attempted to reconcile the Protestants, led by Melanchthon, and the Catholics, represented by Contarini, but without avail.

In 1546 the Schmalkald War broke out, first going against the Protestants, but finally resulted in the "Peace of Augsburg" (1555), when both sides, worn out, were willing to quit fighting, and recognize each other as having a right to exist.

V. ULRICH ZWINGLI (1484-1531).

The Reformation in Switzerland was led by Zwingli. He was a scholarly man, having studied at Basle, Bern and Vienna, and taught Latin at Basle while he studied philosophy. He did not come to the Reformation principles like Luther, by an inner struggle for peace and salvation, but by philosophical and biblical studies. "The time has come when the ancient faith shall be restored according to the Word of God; indulgences are a Roman snare and a delusion." Zwingli went back to the source—to the Scriptures—for authority in religion.

In 1506 Zwingli became pastor at Glarus, where he continued his studies in the classics and philosophy. In 1515 he was chaplain in an Italian campaign, and the next year was transferred to Ensiedlen, where he opposed the indulgences. Through his influence the canton of Zurich refused the papal emissary permission to come there.

In 1521 Pope Leo X. requested the Swiss troops to fight the French; Zwingli opposed this, holding all war for mercenary purposes to be wrong; war is never justified, save for righteousness.

In 1522 the Bishop of Constance made a formal charge against Zwingli and ordered Zurich to silence him. Zwingli answered by sixty-seven theses, or articles, holding the absolute supremacy of Christ; the direct approach to Christ; he rejected the mass; and denounced the hypocrisy of Rome. He invited his enemies to a debate and won in the disputation.

In 1525 his canton threw off the authority of the bishop. Zwingli was throughout a democrat. He was slain in battle in 1531.

VI. CALVIN (1509-1565).

John Calvin was born in Noyon, France; was educated for the priesthood in Paris, and studied law at Bouges and Orleans. He heard from his teacher, Wolmar, the doctrine of salvation by faith taught by Le-

Fevre and Luther. Calvin was a great student, especially adept in the classics. He had a logical mind, and fearlessly thought out his theology. In 1534 he was banished from France. He started for Germany, and accidentally (if accidents happen) met Farel at Geneva. Farel persuaded him to stay at Geneva and help the cause of the Reformation.

In 1536 Calvin published his " Institutes of the Christian Religion." His theology was full-grown at the beginning of his career. As Wiclif was the founder of English prose, Luther of German, so is Calvin of French.

Calvin's genius and natural leadership soon put him at the head of Geneva, whereby the city became completely transformed, even more than Florence under the leadership of Savonarola.

Calvin's theology emphasizes a different side of Christian truth than Luther's. The Catholic Church was a combination of Jewish legalism, and paganism or idolatry. Luther struck at the former with his doctrine of grace, and Calvin at the latter with his high conception of God and the " Divine Decree." He further emphasized predestination, election, total depravity, irresistible grace, and the everlasting perseverance of the elect.

In 1538 there was a revolt against the supreme authority of Calvin and Farel, and they were banished, but were recalled in 1541. The " Ecclesiastical Ordinances " were established, creating the officers of the Church: (1) Pastors, who should explain the Word, and dispense the sacraments. (2) Teachers, of the university and lower schools. (3) Presbyters (elders), who should exercise discipline, visit the members and test their faith. (4) Deacons, who should care for the sick and the poor.

The discipline at Geneva was severe. In five years there were fifty-eight death sentences and seventy-six banishments in a population of 20,000. Servetus was executed in 1553.

The Swiss Reformation, under the leadership of Bullinger, Zwingli's successor, united with the Calvinists in 1549.

VII. ENGLAND.

The Reformation principles had been growing in England since the days of Wiclif and the Lollards. The humanists, Erasmus, Colet and More, were at Oxford.

King Henry VIII. was a loyal Catholic. In 1521 he wrote in defense of the " Seven Sacraments," as a refutation of Luther. The Pope knighted him the " Defender of the Faith."

In 1527 Henry wanted a divorce from his wife, Catherine of Aragon, to marry Anne Boleyn. The pope refused to consent, but Henry was sustained in his action by public sentiment; not that the divorce was right, but that the pope had no authority in the matter. In 1534 the " Supremacy Act " was passed, making the king the head of the Church of England. The Reformation Parliament (1529-36) brought about many other reforms: curtailment of ecclesiastical courts, prohibition of the payment of annates, of appeals to Rome, denial of the pope's authority to appoint bishops, and the suppression of the monasteries.

The Reformation in England made gradual progress under King Edward VI. (1547-53), but had a short reversion under " Bloody Mary " (1553-58). Three hundred persons were burned during her short reign. Ridley, Latimer, Hooper and Cranmer were victims. In Queen Elizabeth's reign (1558-1603) the Romanist legislation of Mary was repealed. The Thirty-nine

Articles were adopted in 1563. In this period the non-conformist Churches have their rise.

VIII. SCOTLAND.

From the early part of the fifteenth century the ideas of Wiclif and Hus were preached in Scotland, and several were burned who had the boldness to preach them. Patrick Hamilton, a strong leader, was martyred in 1528.

John Knox (1505-1572) fled to Geneva (1549) and imbibed Calvinism. In 1555 Knox returned to Scotland, and was largely responsible for the "covenant" which the Protestant nobility made to aid one another (1557). Knox went (1556) to Geneva, but returned to Edinburgh May 2, 1559, and became the acknowledged leader of the Reformation in Scotland. In August, 1560, parliament established Protestantism and abolished Romanism.

Andres Melville (1545-1622) was Knox's successor. He crystallized Scotch Presbyterianism.

IX. OTHER COUNTRIES.

1. **The Reformation** spread rapidly east to Prussia and Poland; north to Denmark,

Norway, Sweden, and Iceland; also to Bohemia, Hungary, and Moravia. In the northern countries Protestantism became supreme; in the southern, the counter-reformation brought about a reversion to Rome.

2. France. Protestantism had no real chance in France. The governments of France and Spain were centralized and organized, and these, being Catholic, were able to crush the new movement. In 1572 was the Massacre of St. Bartholomew, when from 20,000 to 100,000 Protestants were slain in cold blood. In 1598 the Edict of Nantes granted toleration. This was revoked in 1685.

3. The Netherlands. The Dutch were a liberty-loving people, and naturally inclined toward Protestantism. The Spanish Inquisition, under the Duke of Alva, did its worst here; but the Protestants, under William of Orange, gained the day, and Calvinism was established. Arminius (1560-1609) revolted against Calvinistic election and irresistible grace.

The five points of Calvinism and Arminianism became the basis for two schools of theology in Protestantism.

X. THE COUNTER REFORMATION (CATHOLIC CHURCH).

The Council of Trent (1545) cut off all possibility of a reconciliation with the two parties—the Reformers and the Catholics. The Protestants aroused the Catholics to new activities on their part—to stop the abuses and bald corruptions in the Roman Church, and to make a campaign in aggressive as well as defensive Catholicism. Three things mark the strength of the Counter-Reformation which saved Rome and prevented Protestantism from sweeping all before it.

1. The Order of the Jesuits. At each time in the Catholic Church, when she was most in need, a new order came into being and saved her. Ignatius Loyola (1491-1556), the founder of the Jesuits, established the order on the vow of poverty, chastity, and obedience to the pope. The doctrines of the Jesuits were: (1) the end justifies the means. (2) Promises made with a mental reservation may be broken. (3) A distinction between theological and philosophical obedience. These doctrines are subversive to morality and free government.

2. The Council of Trent strengthened the

Catholic Church by uniting their forces and reaffirming their doctrines.

3. The Spanish Inquisition. Ferdinand and Isabella of Spain got the consent of Pope Sixtus IV. (1478) to establish an " Inquisitorial Court " to seek out and punish heretics. The Spanish temperament and fanaticism used this with such severity that even the pope objected, but without avail. Charles V., Emperor, was also King of Spain. He was succeeded by his son, Philip II.

This Spanish Inquisition was invoked by Pope Paul IV. to stamp out Protestantism. It did its work with the most bloody horrors. Protestants were sought, their property confiscated, and they were imprisoned, tortured, and burned. Especially in Spanish territory was its severity felt and Protestantism crushed.

XI. THE THIRTY YEARS' WAR (1618-1648).

The Peace of Augsburg (1555) was a truce between the Catholics and Lutherans, but did not protect the Calvinists. Furthermore, the Counter-Reformation led to persecutions and oppression. In 1608 was formed the "Protestant Union," and the next year the "Catholic League."

The Thirty Years' War had four stages.

1. The Bohemian Period (1618-23). The war was provoked by the Catholics, who tore down a Protestant church and closed another. The Protestants resented this and rebelled. The Bohemian King Ferdinand became emperor, crushed the rebellion and almost uprooted the Reformation in Bohemia.

2. The Danish Period (1625-1629). The Catholic emperor threatened the life of Protestantism. Christian IV., King of Denmark, became the leader of the Protestants, with Count Mansfeld and Christian of Anholt. The Catholic forces were led by Tilly and Wallenstein.

The military genius of Wallenstein was too much for the Protestant forces, which, in the main, lost out. The Edict of Restitution (1629) restored to the Catholics all that the Protestants had gained since 1555.

3. The Swedish Period (1630-35). Gustavus Adolphus, King of Sweden, an enthusiastic Protestant, came to Germany to help the cause. He defeated Tilly twice, and Wallenstein, but lost his own life (1632).

He saved the Protestant cause in Germany from a total overthrow.

4. The French Period (1635-1648). The war would have ended had not France interfered. Richelieu was ambitious for the aggrandizement of France and the overthrow of the House of Austria. He offered aid to the Protestants to continue the war. The miserable war was carried on, more as a struggle for political existence and supremacy than for religious differences. It ended with the Treaty of Westphalia (1648), which granted religious toleration to Catholics, Lutherans, and Calvinists.

XII. THE MEANING OF THE REFORMATION.

The Humanists and the Mystics prepared the way, religiously, by going back to the Bible, and gaining peace without the Roman forms, which made the Reformation possible. But Luther was the creative genius that caused the Reformation. Being a peasant, his religion was full of superstition. He feared the wrath of God. His tremendous struggles of conscience were to appease God's wrath. Finally he came to the doctrine of God's grace. Salvation is nothing else than God's favor; not, as in Paul's case, à moral transformation through faith, but simply a fellowship in God's love and favor regardless of sins in the life. Luther knew he was a sinner, yet held that he was saved, and not a mere candidate for salvation in the future. This present possession was possible, because it depended not upon his own goodness, but on God's grace.

Luther thus broke entirely with the Catholic Church, which he identified with his own peasant religion, and set up "inner experience" as authority, in place of the pope and the hierarchy. The Early Church was interested in the "Person of Christ" (see chapter III), the Mediæval, in "man," and the Reformation in "salvation." This salvation rested on inner experience for its authority. But an external authority was demanded, so Luther substituted the "Bible" for the "Church."

The Reformation meant freedom. This freedom was yet to be won; first religious, then civil freedom. The struggle for the former lasted up to 1648. The latter has been going on ever since, reaching its climax in the French Revolution and the

Huguenots of France, among whom was Helene de la Place, a descendant of Coligny, who was murdered on St. Bartholomew's night. Many Quakers came here from England, as well as refugees from all parts of Germany, who sought and found protection under the mild rule of Count Henry.

III. GEOGRAPHY.

Wittgenstein is a mountainous district between the Rhein and Weser River systems. Near the southwest border is the source of the Eder River (2,100 feet), which flows through the county and empties into the Weser; and also of the Lahn, which flows into the Rhein. The mountains are covered with dense forests, and the valleys are cultivated. This land is secluded, far removed from the streams of commerce and the worldliness of civilization.

Schwarzenau is situated on the Eder, beautifully nestled between the mountains, in one of the quietest and most secluded corners of Germany. Nature and nature's God are the objects of communion and companionship. Even the rulers of this quiet and sequestered spot are pious and religious instead of worldly, as is the custom among their class.

IV. THE PIETISTS OF SCHWARZ-ENAU.

In the archives at Laasphe are five letters, written by the daughter of Count Henry, who lived at Schwarzenau, describing the life and habits of these people. She writes, " They spend their time in Bible study, in prayer, and in deeds of kindness and charity." Count Henry testifies that they were the best Christians that he ever saw, and the most peaceful citizens in Germany.

V. THE BRETHREN.

Bible study and prayer convinced some of them that the will of the Lord could not be carried out unless they organized themselves into a church. Alexander Mack, their leader, describes the origin of the church in the following words: " Finally, in the year 1708, eight persons entered into a covenant with each other, with the help of God, to endeavor to attain to the answer of a good conscience by rendering obedience to all the commands of the Lord Jesus and to follow him as their Good Shepherd and Leader through good and evil report. Those eight persons, of whom five were brethren and three sisters [the names of the brethren were as follows: George Graby and Lucas Fetter, of Hesse Cassel; Alexander Mack, of Schriesheim, in the Palatinate; Andrew Bony, of Basle, in Switzerland; and John Kipping, of Nuerenburg; and the names of the sisters were Joanna Bony, Anna Margaretta Mack, and Joanna Kipping], covenanted with each other as brethren and sisters under the cross of our Lord Jesus Christ, to dwell together in the unity of faith as a society. By consulting history they found that the primitive Christians, in the first and second centuries, uniformly were, according to the command of Christ, planted into the likeness of his death, by a baptism in water by a threefold immersion. Not resting their faith, however, upon the authority of history, they searched the Scriptures of the New Testament and, finding explicit testimony to that import, they became desirous of practicing a means so strongly recommended by the example of our Lord, and emphatically enjoined by his written precept, believing that it became them thus to fulfill all righteousness."

The question of baptism was important. Their leader traveled over Germany and studied the history of the subject. The conclusion of the mode was evident—trine immersion. The little company wanted Mack to be their minister and to baptize them. But he desired to be baptized first. They prayed and fasted and then cast lots to determine which of the four brethren should baptize Mack. The name has been kept secret, "that no one might take occasion to call the society by the name of any man, as was the case with the Corinthian Church."

"The crisis for the camp to move forward was now arrived; they were now made willing in the day of the Lord's power. Accordingly they went out in the morning to a stream called the Eder, and there, he upon whom the lot had fallen, baptized the brother who had discovered so great anxiety to submit to that ordinance; this being done he was now acknowledged as duly qualified; he baptized him first by whom he had been baptized, and the remaining three brethren and three sisters; thus were the eight, at an early hour in the morning, baptized in the water by trine immersion." (Preface to "Rites and Ordinances," by Alexander Mack, ed. 1810.)

VI. THE GROWTH OF THE CHURCH.

The new church was so active in the work of testimony and Bible study that in the short space of seven years their society became numerous, not only at Schwarzenau, but also in the Palatinate and in the Rhein Valley. A society was formed at Marienborn, where all the Brethren of the Palatinate finally gathered because of severe persecution.

Persecutions continued, so that the church at Marienborn was compelled to move, and they all went to Krefeld, in Prussia, about thirty miles northwest of Cologne, near the border of Holland. Missionaries were sent in every direction, who did splendid work converting souls, but persecutions drove them all back to Krefeld and Schwarzenau. Some of the Brethren were beaten, some were imprisoned, and one, Christian Liebe, was forced to serve on the galleys with hardened criminals. These persecutions were endured with wonderful heroism, patience, and unsullied faith and loyalty to the church. The Church of the Brethren was born out of Bible-study, prayer, and the fiery trials of inhuman persecutions.

165

VII. MIGRATIONS.

In the year 1719 Peter Becker, with about forty families, left Krefeld and came to America, settling in Germantown, Pa., and vicinity.

The same year, at Easter, the soldiers at Schwarzenau came to the Brethren and by force wrested the babes from their mothers' arms, and took them to the State Church at Arfeldt and had them sprinkled. About the same time a suit was brought against Count Henry by his cousin at Wetzlar, because Henry was allowing the Brethren (die Tauefer) to remain in his territory against the law of the Treaty of Westphalia. No doubt Henry told the Brethren his predicament, that he could no longer protect them. So in 1720 the Church at Schwarzenau, about forty families, migrated to Westervain, West Friesland, in the north of Holland, west of the Zuider Zee. A letter of Henry to the authorities at Wetzlar, defending himself, states that he did not have "godless" people in his territory, but the best Christians that he ever saw. But they had just left the country, about forty families, and no one was left except Lutherans, Reformed, and Catholics.

The Brethren left Westervain in 1729, and under the leadership of Alexander Mack they came to Germantown, Pa.

VIII. THE CHURCH IN AMERICA.

The Brethren who came from Krefeld with Peter Becker settled in Germantown and in the valley of the Schuylkill. At first no church was organized. In 1723 a false report went abroad, that Elder Christian Liebe, the greatest orator of the Church in Germany, had landed in Philadelphia. The Brethren from the valley came to the city with their neighbors and friends. Although disappointed in not finding Liebe, they were invited into the home of Peter Becker, and a friendship was formed that bore fruit. The Brethren of Germantown made a return visit, which resulted in six conversions. At Christmas, 1723, these six converts, the " first fruits " of the Church in America, applied for baptism. Peter Becker baptized them in the Wissahickon Creek in Germantown. The same Christmas evening they held the first love feast in America in the house of John Gomorry. There were seventeen members residing in Germantown, who with the six new ones celebrated this feast together. The church was also formally organized on that day. Peter Becker was made elder and had charge of the church.

The coming of Mack and the Brethren in 1729 greatly strengthened the cause in Germantown.

IX. MISSIONARY ENDEAVORS.

In 1724 a missionary party of seven horsemen and seven footmen, Peter Becker being leader, left their industries and homes in Germantown and traveled over the surrounding counties to preach the Gospel. They visited the scattered Brethren, held meetings and love feasts in their homes, and baptized the new converts. Martin Urner, the first convert in America, lived at Coventry, near Pottstown. At his home a meeting and love feast were held, and a church was organized—the second in America— with Martin Urner as minister, November 7, 1724.

Five days later, in the home of Heinrich Hoehn, in the Pequea Valley, another meeting was held, which resulted in seven conversions, the last of whom was Conrad Beissel. A few days later two more were baptized. These were formed into the Conestoga congregation, with Beissel as preacher.

X. HERESY AND SCHISM.

Conrad Beissel had a checkered career in Germany and had many peculiar views on religion. Although baptized in 1724 by Peter Becker, and made minister of the Conestoga congregation, he soon began to preach his strange doctrines. He was Jewish in holding to the Sabbath, or seventh day, instead of the Lord's Day; he was a mystic, he believed in celibacy, and the life of the cloister. In 1728 the crisis came; the Conestoga church was divided. He chose seven —the Jewish sabbatic number—whom he baptized thrice backward, to return the baptism to the Brethren which they received from Becker, then forward, to initiate them into the new faith—a faith not unlike the Essenes of the Jews. Beissel founded a monastery at Ephrata, Pa., and used all his ingenuity and tireless efforts to destroy the Brethren congregations and to make proselytes from other churches.

The Ephrata Society was founded in 1732. It was under Beissel's management and influence. Three classes of persons composed the society: the married people, the unmarried brothers, or monks, and the virgins or sisters.

In 1738-9 there was an exodus from Germantown to Ephrata, largely brought about by the visions and mysticism of Stephen Koch, who aroused an interest in this mystic life as a higher type of godliness. The various congregations of the Brethren lost heavily through this spiritistic, mystical, and monastic fanaticism.

XI. OTHER CHURCHES OF THE BRETHREN.

We have already mentioned the founding of the Coventry and the Conestoga congregations in 1724. In 1733 the Great Swamp congregation was organized in Bucks County, and the Amwell church in New Jersey. The Oley congregation had members as early as 1732, when Peter Becker held services there. The White Oak congregation, of Lancaster County, Pa., was organized in 1736; the Little Conewago church in 1738, and the Conewago church in 1741, both of York County, Pa. In 1752 was founded the Great Swatara congregation, and the Little Swatara in 1757. The Northkill church in Berks County, Pa., about fifteen miles from Reading, came into existence about 1748. Near York, Pa., the Codorus congregation, made up largely of emigrants from the eastern churches, was organized about 1758. About the middle of the century some Brethren crossed the Alleghanies to Brothers Valley, in Somerset County, Pa. From here they went to Stony Creek, Bedford County, where the church was organized soon after 1762. In 1760 the church was begun in Middletown Valley, Md., and in 1780 in Daleville, Va., and at Flat Rock, Shenandoah Co., about five years earlier.

XII. LEADERS IN THE CHURCH OF THE BRETHREN.

1. Alexander Mack. Alexander Mack was the founder of the Church of the Brethren, in that he was the leader, baptizer, and minister of the small group of eight persons who covenanted together to restore apostolic Christianity in Schwarzenau in 1708, and to promote the kingdom of God and his glory. Mack was in the fullest sense the " restorer " of apostolic Christianity by going to the New Testament and to history to find the truth of the Gospel and the practice of the early Church, and making these the only creed of the Church.

Mack was born in 1689, at Schriesheim,

Germany, of good parents who had wealth and great piety. He was a great evangelist and leader. His wise counsel seems always to have been respected, and his superb Christian character held in the highest esteem. His wealth was spent in charity and his whole life was devoted to the cause of the kingdom. When the persecutions compelled them to leave Schwarzenau he led his flock to Holland, and later to Germantown, Pa. Here he spent his last days, and died February 19, 1735. His body now lies in the Brethren cemetery back of the church in Germantown.

2. **Johannes Naas.** Elder Naas was an eloquent preacher and had great influence in the Church, next to Mack. He joined the Church in Marienborn and migrated with the Church to Krefeld, where he was elder of the congregation. He suffered great persecutions, especially by the officers of the government, who tried to force him, because of his great stature and fine physique, to join the king's guard. He endured all kinds of torture, but he declared that he had enlisted in the services of his King, Jesus Christ, and he resolved to be loyal to his Master. The King of Prussia honored him

for his loyalty and sent him away with a reward.

When Christian Liebe caused factions in the church at Krefeld, Elder Naas showed the highest Christian charity and forbearance. He came to America in 1733. His missionary work in the Rhein Valley deserves widespread recognition. His eloquence, his zeal, and his piety are a rich inheritance to posterity.

3. Peter Becker. Peter Becker was a minister in Krefeld, who became the leader of the migration of forty families, 200 persons, to Germantown in 1719. He was born in Dillsheim, Germany, in 1687, joined the Church in Krefeld in 1714, and died in Skippack, Pa., in 1758.

Becker was an expert weaver and had Conrad Beissel in his home a year as apprentice. He was ordained elder on Christmas, 1723, when the church in Germantown was formally organized. The same day he baptized the six new converts, the " first fruits " in America, and presided at the first love feast that same eventful evening. He was a wise elder, a good counselor, and during the trying times of the Beissel schism, he directed the Church with rare patience and statesmanship. Becker was an enthusiastic missionary, and organized the churches at Coventry and Conestoga in 1724. He was not an eloquent preacher, but he was fervent in prayer, and in song, and exemplary in the Christian life.

4. **Alexander Mack, Jr.,** was born in Schwarzenau January 25, 1712, and was baptized in Holland in 1728, the year before he came to America. His religious earnestness made him susceptible to the mysticism of Koch, who induced him to go with him to the Wissahickon, where they lived for a year in a hut in pious prayer and meditation. In 1738 he went with Koch to Ephrata, but in 1748 we find him back in Germantown in full fellowship with the Brethren, who placed upon Mack and Christopher Saur the oversight of the church. From now on he gave fifty-five years of continuous, loyal, and efficient service to the Church of the Brethren. Mack was fully ordained elder June 10, 1753. He was one of the greatest writers of colonial America, having a large correspondence, as well as the writer of many pamphlets and a great number of poems and hymns. He died March 20, 1803.

5. Christopher Saur, the printer, was in every sense a leader of the early Brethren. He was born in Laasphe, Wittgenstein, in Westphalia, Germany. Here is the castle of Count Henry, whose sovereignty extended over Schwarzenau. There is some circumstantial evidence that he moved to Berleburg, where we have a record of Saur families, some of whom were printers. Saur's press later on came from Berleburg.

Saur came to America in 1724 with his wife and son, and finally settled in Germantown. He was a man of great versatility. An early record says of him, " Saur is a very ingenious man. He is a separatist, who has become dexterous in at least thirty trades; for, having come over to America as a tailor, he has since become a printer, apothecary, surgeon, botanist, clock and watchmaker, cabinet maker, book binder, newspaper maker, manufacturer of his own tools, wire and lead drawer, paper maker, etc., etc." (Quoted from Brumbaugh.)

In 1731 he built a large house, 60 x 60 feet, which was used for the Brethren meetinghouse. In 1738 he received his printing outfit from Berleburg. The same year he printed an almanac, and soon developed a large printing business. In 1743 he published the first edition of the Bible—the first Bible in a European tongue printed in America. Two other editions of the Bible followed this, in 1763 and 1776. Saur also printed the first German newspaper in America, August 20, 1739. He died in 1758, and the work was then carried on by his son.

6. **Christopher Saur, Jr.,** wrote in his diary, "I was born on the 26th of September, 1721, in the town of Laasphe, in Wittgenstein, about six hours from Marburg." He came to America with his parents in 1724, went with them to Lancaster County, Pa., and returned to Germantown in 1731. At the age of fifteen he became a member of the Church of the Brethren. "I was born anew through holy baptism on the 24th of February, 1737." Ten years after this he was elected deacon, and a year later he was called to the ministry and received the joint oversight of the church with the younger Mack. Five years later he was fully ordained to the eldership.

At the death of the elder Saur, Christopher, Jr., became proprietor of the estate and manager of the printing business. He continued the publications, which had now become one of the greatest factors in our colonial civilization. He published the second and third editions of the Bible (1763 and 1776), and the first religious magazine in America, called " Geistliche Magazin."

Holding firmly to the non-resisting and non-swearing principles of the Brethren, he was persecuted and most shamefully treated during the Revolutionary War, and his property was confiscated. His opposition to slavery also made him enemies. But his Christian fortitude and patience through evil days are unsurpassed in the annals of Christendom. He had a family of nine children. He died August 26, 1784.

The sources for the Church of the Brethren have been my own study of the Pietistic Movement in Marburg, Germany; my researches in the archives at Laasphe; and for the Church in America I had to rely entirely on the work of others, Dr. Brumbaugh's " History of the Brethren," and also the work of Elder G. N. Falkenstein, and " Two Centuries of the Brethren." These works must be consulted for a full treatment of the subject.

THE CHURCH OF THE BRETHREN

QUESTIONS.

1. Describe the Pietistic Movement; sects. Why were they persecuted?

2. Where did these persecuted Pietists go for refuge? Whence did they come?

3. Describe the natural features of Schwarzenau. What effect does nature have on religion?

4. Describe the piety of the people at Schwarzenau.

5. Describe the beginning of the Church of the Brethren. Who was their leader? What was the year? What was their creed?

6. Tell of the growth of the Church in Germany. What were their experiences?

7. Describe the migrations of the Church.

8. What three things happened in Germantown, Pa., December 25, 1723?

9. Describe the missionary activities of the Church in America.

10. Describe the Ephrata movement. Who were Beissel and Koch?

11. Name some of the early churches founded by the Brethren.

12. Name six leaders of the Church of the Brethren. Tell of their zeal, their piety, deeds, and character.

CHAPTER X.

From Kant to the Present, 1780——— A. D.

I. INTRODUCTION.

In the year 1780 Immanuel Kant, the great philosopher, published his "Critique of Pure Reason." This meant a new era in philosophy, and simultaneous changes in political, social, scientific, and religious thinking.

Politically, nations were struggling for civil liberty. America was in the throes of the Revolution. France was about to storm the Bastille and begin the reign of terror. All Europe was in commotion through the Napoleonic wars—the birth-pangs of civil rights. Greece got her independence from Turkey in 1831. Germany was consolidated under William I. in 1870. France became a republic. Italy the same year became a nation. All civilized nations made strides toward constitutional governments.

Science was set free, and the astronomers,

the geologists, the biologists revolutionized man's view of the world. In 1859 appeared Darwin's " Origin of Species," which attempted to prove scientifically what Kant had already taught—the law of evolution.

Philosophy was forced by the skepticism of the eighteenth century to reëxamine its foundations and tenets. Everything was criticised, reëxamined, and studied in the light of science and history. All history was rewritten from the new point of view. The nineteenth century produced a new race of historians, who wrote our classic histories of Greece, Rome, France, Holland, England, America, and of the Christian Church. Education was made popular and general.

Japan was opened (1854) to the civilization of the West and was literally born again. China has been awakened from her long sleep by a century of missionary prayers and endeavors.

Science and invention, during this period, gave the world the steamboat, the railroad, the telegraph, the telephone, all electrical appliances, the airship, modern warships, the development of international diplomacy; and thus time and space have been eliminated and the world has been brought together as a family. We cannot understand the history of the Church nor her present problems without a clear vision of life as a whole.

II. THE ROMAN CATHOLIC CHURCH.

The Roman Church has largely taken the attitude of opposition to this rapid advance in culture. Nevertheless, the Church has grown rapidly, and has become better organized and narrower in her theological thinking. Three principal things mark the changes in the Catholic Church: (1) Opposition to the use of Bibles by the masses, and to the reading of modern scientific literature; (2) the proclamation of the dogma of the " Immaculate Conception " by Pope Pius IX. in 1854; and (3) the dogma of the " Infallibility of the Pope," which was proclaimed at the twentieth and last Œcumenical Council in 1870. The pope considers himself a prisoner in the Vatican, because the so-called " Papal States " are now governed by the King of Italy against the will of the pope.

III. MISSIONARY ENTERPRISE.

This epoch is the greatest missionary epoch since the first century of the Christian

Church. Before 1780 there were only a few missionary societies; viz., the Christian Faith Society for the West Indies, 1691; the Society for the Promotion of Christian Knowledge, 1698; the Society for the Promotion of the Gospel, 1701; and the Moravian Missionary Society, 1732.

Through the influence of Carey, the Baptist Missionary Society was founded in 1792. Then followed in rapid succession the London Missionary Society, 1795; the Scottish Society, 1796; the Church Missionary Society, 1799; the Religious Tract Society, the same year; the British and Foreign Bible Society in 1804; the London Society for the Promotion of Christianity Among the Jews, 1808; the American Board of Foreign Missions (Congregational), 1810; Wesleyan Missionary Society, 1813; General Baptist, 1817; American Bible Society, 1816; the Methodist Episcopal Church Missionary Society, 1819; the Presbyterian Church in the United States, 1837.

Today there are over a hundred large societies and several hundred smaller ones engaged in the propagation of the Gospel among the heathen and the needy. The missionary work has developed along all

lines and has for practical purposes sub-
divided itself into: (1) Evangelistic, the
preaching of the Word; (2) educational,
teaching the children and the natives in the
schools and colleges; (3) literary, the dis-
tribution of Bibles, tracts, and religious literature with the hope that the truth will
make its own appeal; (4) medical, the estab-
lishment of hospitals and dispensaries, and
the visiting of physicians and nurses to al-
leviate human suffering; (5) and in some
places the industrial work, teaching the natives a useful trade, especially the building
arts. The one aim in all these efforts is to
bring men TO CHRIST, and to build them
up IN CHRIST. It is also recognized that
the principal work of the missionary is to
train the native pastors who will eventually
do the work of evangelizing.

The nineteenth century has opened the
doors of the world to the missionary enterprise. The successes have been inspiring,
but the task yet remaining challenges the
faith and energy of the Church.

IV. DENOMINATIONS.

The Reformation brought forth several
denominations—Lutheran, Reformed, Pres-

byterian, the Church of England (Protestant Episcopal in America), and the Anabaptist sects of Switzerland, which were the forerunners of the Mennonites and the Baptists. These last also greatly influenced the Separatists of a later day. The Congregational church grew out of the Puritans, who separated themselves from the Church of England about 1580 under the leadership of Robert Browne. They became Pilgrims to Holland, came to America in the Mayflower in 1620, and have remained the dominant church in New England. In 1805 a number of Congregational churches, together with Harvard University, formed the Unitarian Church.

The Friends began with the preaching of George Fox in 1647. Because of severe persecutions they fled to Holland, Germany, and America. William Penn founded the colony of Pennsylvania, which became an asylum for kindred spirits, especially the Mennonites, who came to Germantown in 1683, and the Brethren who came in 1719.

The Methodist Church was founded by John Wesley, whose movement for a deeper spiritual life began in 1729. John and Charles Wesley and George Whitefield were ordained ministers in the Church of England, who had no thought of leaving their church, but they tried to attain greater holiness and spiritualize the church. Wesley declared on his death bed that he had lived and would die a member of the Church of England. But the movement which he inaugurated was not incorporated by the church, and thus it became a separate church. The Methodist Church in America has seventeen branches and numbers (1910) over six and a half millions. The Baptists (fifteen bodies) number about a million less. The Lutherans in America (twenty-three bodies) have two and a quarter millions; the Presbyterians (twelve bodies) number about two millions; the Disciples of Christ have one and one half millions.

V. THEOLOGY OF THE NINETEENTH CENTURY.

The new point of view in philosophy and history, the skepticism of the eighteenth century, and the new science compelled innovations in theology.

1. Germany. In Germany, Schleiermacher did most to bring men of culture back to religion, and to define religion in a skeptical age. He held that religion is based on the feelings and is therefore independent of philosophy. All higher culture, music, art, and poetry are based on the feelings, and therefore have a religious foundation. Schleiermacher's personal magnetism, his eloquence, and his great scholarship made him the pathfinder of a new era in theology.

Strauss published his "Life of Christ" in 1835. His conclusions were untenable, for he held that Jesus was a myth, that he did not really live as the Gospels picture him. Strauss held further that we do not need this historic Christ for religion, but only the ideas which we possess in the Gospels. The danger of this teaching was in the claim that a careful study of the Scriptures would substantiate his theory. This forced the theological world to make a critical study of the Bible to defend its truths. Thus the "critical," or scientific study of the Bible was launched.

The Ritschlian theology of Germany attempted, like Schleiermacher, to make religion independent of philosophy and metaphysics, and base it on experience. This opened the way to the most critical study of the Bible while retaining religious piety.

This school has had a great influence in Germany, England and America.

2. England. Samuel Taylor Coleridge (1772-1834) studied in Germany and brought to England the broader theology prevailing there. The Broad Church Movement attempted to be up to date in the philosophic thought of the day, and so to emphasize the vital and fundamental doctrines of religion only so as to make the Church broad enough to include all evangelical Christians, regardless of their doctrinal points of view. The greatest men of this movement were Richard Whately (1787-1863), Thomas Arnold (1795-1842), F. D. Maurice (1805-1872), Charles Kingsley (1819-1875), A. P. Stanley (1815-1881), H. H. Milman (1791-1868), F. W. Robertson (1816-1863), F. W. Farrar (1831-1903). This Broad Church Party strongly emphasized social improvement and practical religion.

The Low Church Party also was a reaction against the ecclesiasticism of the High Church and was characterized by its evangelistic interest in contrast to the theological or sacramental. It sought to accomplish fruit in the everyday lives of men. The leaders were William Romaine, John

Newton, Robert Cecil, Thomas Scott, William Wilberforce, and William Cowper, the poet.

The Oxford Movement was an Anglo-Catholic movement, a reaction against the Broad Church and the new theology. It is also called the "Tractarian Movement," because of the tracts that were written to propagate the cause. The leaders of the movement were Keble, Froude, Church, Newman, and Pusey. In 1841 Newman published "Tract Number Ninety," which tried to prove that the Church of England was a part of the Roman Catholic Church. This brought forth the crisis which caused the separation of many who went over to the Roman Church. John Henry Newman was no doubt the greatest of the leaders. His problem was largely the question of authority, which he could not find in the TRUTH as revealed in the Scriptures and in reason, which he distrusted, but in the pope. He became a cardinal in the Roman Church, and was followed by Manning. "In 1852 Oxford lost ninety-two members, sixty-three of whom were divines; Cambridge lost forty-three, nineteen of whom were divines. In 1862 the number had increased to 867, of whom 243 were divines. It included almost exclusively persons of note—military men and nobles, members of Parliament and men in the professions." (Moncrief, p. 441.)

3. America. In the eighteenth century Jonathan Edwards (1703-1758) and his successors preached Calvinism in its extreme form—infant damnation, the wrath of an angry God, and predestination. In the nineteenth century a new epoch of New England theology was ushered in by Horace Bushnell (1802-1876). Bushnell opposed the Edwardian theology and upheld the freedom of the will in religion as well as in politics. As opposed to infant corruption until a revival-conversion, he advocated " Christian nurture," which brings up the child from the beginning as belonging to God, so that it never knows any different. Against the tritheism of the orthodoxy of the day, he interpreted the trinity as a moral and spiritual triunity. Over against a mediæval scholasticism of dry theologies, he advocated a religion of the Spirit and of life.

VI. THE SUNDAY-SCHOOL.

This period has seen the development of the Sunday-school from mere beginnings to its present position of influence and power.

The first Sunday-school in the world, along modern lines, was established by the Church of the Brethren in Germantown, Pa., in 1738. Two years later a school was started in Ephrata, Pa. In 1744 Christopher Saur, in Germantown, published Sunday-school cards for the children, containing appropriate verses.

In 1780 Robert Raikes, in England, gathered the children off the streets of his city and hired teachers to instruct them on Sunday in reading, writing, spelling, and the catechism. Raikes was an editor, and consequently published the work of his school in his paper, the " Gloucester Journal." The papers of London took up the matter and popularized it. The idea was taken up and widely adopted by the churches.

On January 11, 1791, in Philadelphia, a society was formed for the " institution and support of First Day or Sunday-schools." Several Sunday-school unions were formed in Philadelphia and New York in 1816 and 1817. On May 24, 1824, the "American Sunday-school Union " was formed. The first national convention of this Union met in

New York in 1832. In 1872 the National Convention of the American Sunday-school Union adopted the uniform lesson system. In 1875 the convention became international in scope. The first " World's Sunday-school Convention " was held in London in 1889. The statistics for the seventh world's convention (1913) shows the Sunday-school in 205 nations, provinces, or islands. The total enrollment is 28,701,489. The Sunday-schools number 297,866; officers and teachers, 2,624,896; scholars all ages, 26,076,593.

VII. THE CHURCH OF THE BRETHREN.

After the Revolutionary War the Brethren migrated westward into the new territory that was opened to settlement. Most of the new churches were founded by the colonization method. In recent years this has been done extensively in Oklahoma, the Dakotas, and western Canada.

Three great factors have been developed in the Church of the Brethren during the last half of the nineteenth century—the publishing, the educational, and the missionary interests.

Before 1850 Elder Henry Kurtz, recognizing the fact that the church could make no permanent progress without the help of the press, urged the publication of a church paper. The first copy of his " Monthly Gospel Visitor " appeared April 1, 1851. Five years afterwards Elder James Quinter was associated with Elder Kurtz. In rapid succession other papers came before the public with varied success.

The " Pilgrim " appeared January 1, 1870, published by Elders J. B. and H. B. Brumbaugh, of Huntingdon, Pa. This was consolidated with the " Primitive Christian," the successor of the " Gospel Visitor," and thus formed the " Primitive Christian and Pilgrim."

" Der Brüderbote " was started by Lewis A. Plate in 1875. Elder J. T. Myers joined him and the paper was printed part English and part German, and called " Brethren's Messenger." This English part was moved to Lanark, Ill., in 1876, and published thereafter under the name " Brethren at Work," by J. H. Moore, J. T. Myers and M. M. Eshelman. This was consolidated with the " Primitive Christian " in 1883, and called " The Gospel Messenger."

The educational development of this same period was no less remarkable. In 1861 Elder S. Z. Sharp opened a school at Kishacoquillas, Pa., which was truly the forerunner of later schools and colleges. On April 17, 1876, Juniata College was founded at Huntingdon, Pa., by Prof. Zuck. Mt. Morris College began in 1879; Bridgewater in 1880; McPherson in 1887; Daleville in 1890; Lordsburg in 1891; North Manchester in 1895; Elizabethtown in 1898; Blue Ridge in 1899; and Bethany Bible School in 1905. Other schools have been started and have discontinued. Their multiplicity shows the rapid development of interest in education.

The first foreign missionary went to Denmark in 1876. The larger foreign missionary enterprise began in 1894, when Elder W. B. Stover and wife went to India. The work was started in Bulsar in 1895. It has developed so that now (1913) there are nine stations, fifty-eight sub-stations, six organized churches, 1,125 members, 140 native workers, eighty-one village schools with an enrollment of 1,425 pupils.

The Brethren began mission work in China in 1908 in the Shansi Province. This work is being enlarged annually, and the outlook is encouraging. The entire missionary force under the control of the General Mission Board numbers about sixty.

VIII. CHURCH UNION AND UNITY.

The nineteenth century experienced many divisions of churches into new denominations. Some of these divisions were caused by the Civil War; others, through personal ambitions, theological differences, and religious peculiarities. There have been for the last two decades much effort and agitation to bring about " church union." No progress has been made in lessening the number of denominations, but great advances have been made in unity of spirit, and coöperation in moral and social endeavors. Sunday-school and missionary conventions have done much to unite all evangelical bodies into a unity of spirit, thus emphasizing their agreements rather than their differences. While church unity, not union, has been gaining ground, nevertheless each denomination seems to reëmphasize its own peculiar doctrines, thinking thus to do most to enrich the religious life as a whole.

The Church of the Brethren suffered a loss in 1881-1882 by the separation of about

CONCLUSION

8,000 members—the Progressive and the Old Order Brethren. The former have been growing and have now about 20,000 members. They also own the college at Ashland, Ohio. The Old Order Brethren have been losing ground. They have no colleges, Sunday-schools, or missions.

IX. CONCLUSION.

The study of Church history shows the constant power of the Gospel of Christ to transform human life, and at the same time it shows the weakness of humanity to appropriate this Gospel and propagate it in its purity throughout the world. Lessing once said, " Christianity has been a failure, but the religion of Jesus Christ has never been tried." Christianity has not been a failure, although the Church as an organization, whose duty it was to incarnate the religion of Jesus Christ, has many blots upon her record. Nevertheless the true historian must recognize that the Church has always represented the highest ethics and ideals of life that were taught in that particular age. The Church has also fostered education, and almost all the schools in Christendom were founded through her influence. The individuals of the Church have fallen far short of the ethics set for them, but the Church has always preached a sinless Christ as the Way, the Truth, and the Life.

The history of the last nineteen centuries would be an insoluble enigma without a knowledge of the history of the Church. In fact, for many centuries the history of the Church is the history of Europe. Our present creeds, forms, practices, and standards of life can only be understood in the light of their historic origin and development. We must know history to understand our present duty; but we should be free to apply the truth to our own age, untrammeled by the icy hand of the past, which too oft throttles the living present and the unborn future.

QUESTIONS.

1. What event marks the opening of this era? What kind of changes were taking place in public thought?

2. Name three changes in the Roman Church during this period.

3. Describe the progress of missionary endeavors. What kinds of missionary work are done on the fields?

4. What denominations existed at the close of the Reformation? Name some denominations that came into being since the Reformation.

QUESTIONS

5. Who was the leader of theological thought in Germany at the beginning of the century? What was the Broad Church Movement in England? The Low Church Movement? The Oxford Movement? What religious changes took place in America?

6. When and where was the first Sunday-school in the world? Describe the progress of the Sunday-school.

7. In what three ways did the Church of the Brethren develop most during the nineteenth century? Tell something of each.

8. What is the difference between Church "union" and Church "unity"? What progress was made in each?

9. Give two reasons for the study of Church history.